China
Through
Western Eyes
The Twentieth Century

A READER IN HISTORY

China
Through
Western Eyes

The Twentieth Century

A READER IN HISTORY

J.A.G. Roberts

Principal Lecturer in History
The Polytechnic of Huddersfield

ALAN SUTTON

First Published in the United Kingdom in 1992 by
Alan Sutton Publishing Limited
Phoenix Mill · Far Thrupp · Stroud · Gloucestershire

First Published in the United States of America in 1992 by
Alan Sutton Publishing Inc · Wolfeboro Falls · NH · 03896–0848

British Library Cataloguing in Publication Data

Roberts, J.A.G. (John Anthony George), *1935–*
China Through Western Eyes : The Twentieth Century.
I. Title 951

ISBN 0 86299 829 8

Library of Congress Cataloging in Publication Data

China through western eyes. The twentieth century · a reader in
history (edited by) J.A.G. Roberts.
p. cm.
Includes bibliographical references and index.
ISBN 0–86299–829–8 : £7.95 ($14.00 U.S.)
1. China – History – 20th century. 2. China – Foreign public opinion.
3. Public opinion – Europe. 4. Public opinion – United States. I.
Roberts, J.A.G., 1935–.
DS774.C4416 1992
951.05–dc20

Cover picture: 'The Dragon Turns', from *Punch*,
28 December 1927

Typeset in 10/12 Ehrhardt.
Typesetting and origination by
Alan Sutton Publishing Limited.
Printed in Great Britain by
The Guernsey Press Co. Ltd, Guernsey, C.I.

For my father
Frederick G. Roberts

CONTENTS

INTRODUCTION: WESTERN SOURCES ON CHINA IN THE TWENTIETH CENTURY

The purpose of this anthology is to provide a selection of readings from western sources which offer insights into the history of China in the twentieth century. The selection is made from the many books which have appeared in English and it does not include extracts from works written in other European languages or from other printed sources, for example newspapers.

These books are the records of observers of China. Who were these observers? They may be divided into two categories: those who lived and worked in China, at least for a major part of their lives, and those who visited China but were not based there.

The social élite of the residents were the diplomats and members of the consular service, for example, on the British side, Sir Meyrick Hewlett and Reginald F. Johnston, and among the Americans Paul Reinsch. There were the businessmen, represented by the indefatigable writer J.O.P. Bland, by O.D. Rasmussen and by the American Carl Crow. Missionaries contributed their share, though their role as reporters on China was less prominent than in previous centuries – they included the Revds Roland Allen, Archibald Glover, E.J. Hardy, J. Macgowan, W.A.P. Martin and Arthur Smith. Among the residents were a few journalists who lived in China, the best-known of whom at the beginning of the century was George Morrison of *The Times*. Finally, there were those who worked for the Chinese government and its agencies, in particular employees of the Imperial Maritime Customs and those engaged in education.

The other category was that of visitors, who may also be divided into groups. Some were itinerant writers, among them Somerset Maugham, W.H. Auden and Harold Acton; others were philosophers, including John Dewey, Bertrand Russell, Hermann Keyserling and André Malraux. Scholars formed a large group: it was in the first decade of the twentieth century that academics, particularly from American universities, began to make study tours and field trips to China and to use their observations as the basis for a book. Among them may be noted Margaret Burton, John Lossing Buck, J.K. Galbraith and Claudie Broyelle. As the century progressed, and particularly in times of war, many journalists went to China and later turned their reports into books. As for tourists, at first only the most adventurous of the breed – men like Harry Franck, known by his publishers as 'the prince of vagabonds' – reached China. But in the 1960s tourism became big business and travel books, written by tourists or aimed at the tourist market, began to proliferate.

What principles have guided the making of this selection? Preference has been given to accounts which derive from first-hand experience and special attention has been given to those writers who had exceptional opportunities to contribute to the historical record. For example, when Anna Louise Strong went to Changsha in July 1927, she noted that, 'Where the recognised government itself could not investigate, I, as a foreigner with an American passport, could go with ease.'[1] In 1937 Nym Wales, Edgar Snow's wife, spent five months at Yenan, the Chinese Communists' wartime capital. She found that the Communists had lost nearly all their records on the Long March and that she was the only person there who was comprehensively gathering historical information.[2] Alan Winnington was the first European to travel among the Norsu, a minority group living in south-west China formerly known under the pejorative name of Lolo. He arrived at the exact moment when slavery had been abolished and traditional society overthrown. He remarked simply, 'Nobody will ever again be able to see them as I saw them.'[3]

Other writers, too, had unique experiences. Otto Braun was the *only* westerner to take part in the Long March. But his eyewitness qualification was modified by three factors which affected his reporting: at first he was ignorant of Chinese language, history and culture; his diary was lost on the Long March and he had to reconstruct his record; and, on his own admission, he was ideologically motivated, for he declared, 'I look upon my notes as a weapon with which to expose the Maoist manipulators of history and to promote the politico-ideological struggle against Maoism.'[4]

William Geddes's unique experience was of a different kind and it illustrated an advantage of being a foreign observer. In 1936 the village of Kaihsienkung in Chekiang had been the subject of the classic study by Fei Hsiao-tung, *Peasant Life in China*. Twenty years later Geddes was allowed to make a brief visit to the same village to investigate and report on the social changes which had occurred. But when Fei Hsiao-tung returned to Kaihsienkung the following year and published his findings on the changes, these were denounced as 'a plot to restore bourgeois sociology' and he spent a year undergoing corrective labour.

Which westerners were best qualified to air their views on China? Should their length of residence be taken into consideration? W.A. Cornaby once quoted Herbert Spencer's *Study of Sociology* referring to a Frenchman,

> who, having been three weeks in England, proposed to write a book on English characteristics, who after three months found that he was not quite ready, and who, after three years, concluded that he knew nothing about it.

Cornaby applied this formula to visitors to China to explain why 'Old China Hands', as long-time residents in the treaty ports were apt to call themselves, were reluctant to go into print, and why visitors frequently did. He remarked that travel revealed the differences between one race and another, whereas residence revealed the similarities beneath all externals.[5]

Not all writers on China obeyed this rule: some residents, like J.O.P. Bland and the missionary Revd A.E. Moule, had spent many years in China and regarded their long service there as their main qualification for writing on the subject. It is true that some visitors wrote books based on very brief encounters. Geddes's visit to Kaihsienkung referred to above lasted only three and a half days. He admitted that this time was ridiculously short, but pointed out that he could not extend it, and added that his observations were based on Fei's earlier study, that he had reliable assistants and that he had crammed in as much observation as possible within the time available. He justified publishing his findings on the grounds that there was a dearth of first-hand information on developments in the Chinese countryside.[6]

Another qualification for writing was knowledge of China through proficiency in Chinese. However, some influential writers, among them the journalists George Morrison and Harrison Salisbury, knew little or no Chinese. Few writers were prepared to be as frank about the limits to their qualifications as was Peter Fleming in *One's Company*:[7]

WARNING TO THE READER

The recorded history of Chinese civilization covers a period of four thousand years. The population of China is estimated at 450 millions. China is larger than Europe.

The author of this book is twenty-six years old. He has spent, altogether, about seven months in China. He does not speak Chinese.

Fleming, like many others, relied on an interpreter. Simone de Beauvoir argued that this did not present an insuperable obstacle to arriving at a well-informed opinion. She had an official interpreter, a Mr Tsai. But, she said, 'in China an interpreter is not a detective', and added:

If Tsai accompanies me, it is because, without him, I am deaf, dumb, lost: he is a necessity to me. But he is not under instructions to erect fences around me or to sieve the remarks made by people I meet. Never once was my freedom of movement hindered. . . . When our visits were prepared in advance, this was not concealed from us. . . . No, they did not hide China behind their backs, they had not daubed hundreds of villages with stage paint or draped camouflage nets over thousands of miles of countryside; they had us see China.[8]

Western observers may also be distinguished in terms of the range of their observation. Most westerners lived in or had visited the treaty ports, the main cities and areas of European activity. Few went off the beaten track, although, according to Edward Dingle, even in 1910 such travel was less hazardous than might be supposed. He was of the opinion that it was easier for an European to walk through China than it would be for two Chinese, dressed as Chinese, to walk through Great Britain or America. What, he asked, would the canny High-lander or the rural English rustic think of two pigtailed men tramping through their countryside. He crossed China on foot and reached parts of Yünnan previously unvisited by Europeans, but the value of his account was reduced because of his ignorance of Chinese, and because he gloried in the purely private purpose of his trip:

> My sole object in going to China was a personal desire to see China from the inside. My trip was undertaken for no other purpose. I carried no instruments (with the exception of an aneroid), and did not even make a single survey of the untrodden country through which I occasionally passed.[9]

A perennial problem for western writers on China has been how to present a balanced view. W.H. Auden and Christopher Isherwood reported on the beginning of the Sino–Japanese War. Auden was aware of the need for balance and likened himself to a 'neutral, unjudging bird' looking down on the Bad Earth. But in the book neither he nor Isherwood attempted to balance their left-wing views. Sven Lindqvist, a Swedish student who was in Peking from 1961 to 1962, did struggle hard to present an even-handed picture of China after the Great Leap Forward. He explained why the Swedish view of China was so confusingly ambivalent:

> One traveller comes back from China, stimulated, rejuvenated, enthusiastic, as if he has just had a good sail in a stiff breeze. The next one comes back critical, worried, frightened. Someone else has gone from one factory to another and has seen production increas-ing by leaps and bounds. . . . He has met cheerful people, ready to make sacrifices. Another visitor describes the people as indifferent, says their loyalty is forced. He has seen great slag heaps of scrap iron

piled up outside abandoned factories. He describes the deathly stillness of the industrial battlefield and says that China is summoning her last resources in order to survive.

Lindqvist offered a rational explanation for these discrepancies: the Chinese economy worked on a very narrow margin – a small variation in output could make the difference between investment and disastrous shortage. In China things changed very rapidly, and for a visitor to offer a three-dimensional view of China, he must have stayed there long enough to observe change. So, to resolve discrepancies, Lindqvist suggested solemnly:

> Faced with two completely different reports on China the discerning reader should enquire whether both writers were in China simultaneously, for the same length of time, and whether they understood Chinese. Considerations like these will account for most of the discrepancies in their reports.[10]

From the beginning of the twentieth century, visitors to China have included in their number academic or professional persons. Such people were aware that their limited acquaintance with China put them at a disadvantage when it was compared with that of the Old China Hands. In their defence they pleaded the value of their professional expertise. The special ability of the comparative sociologist to span the cultural gap was argued by Dr Edward Ross, Professor of Sociology at the University of Wisconsin:

> The theory, dear to literary interpreters of the Orient, that owing to diversity in mental constitution the yellow man and the white man can never comprehend or sympathize with one another, will appeal little to those who from their comparative study of societies have gleaned some notion of what naturally follows from isolation, the acute struggle for existence, ancestor worship, patriarchal authority, the subjection of women, the decline of militancy, and the ascendancy of scholars.[11]

In the preface to Olga Lang's *Chinese Family and Society*, Karl Wittfogel weighed up the relative value of foreign and 'native' observation:

The disadvantages of a study initiated by a foreigner are obvious. Less obvious are its advantages. The foreign observer is not hampered by the psychological biases which may at times block or even completely frustrate a 'native' study. There is, of course, the danger of replacing native prejudices with imported ones, for the visitor is apt to see the society he is examining as a replica of his own. If this danger is avoided by methodological alertness and self-criticism, the foreign investigator is given an unusual opportunity to make a productive analysis.[12]

A few writers, who combined long residence with extensive study and research, have a permanent place in the literature on China. Reginald Johnston, the District Officer of the British territory of Weihaiwei, studied the social customs of the area where he worked. He argued that the time for generalizations about China had passed:

> . . . China is too vast a country to be adequately described by any one writer or group of writers, and the more we know about China and its people the more strongly we shall feel that future workers must confine themselves to less ambitious objects of study than the whole Empire. The pioneer who with his prismatic compass passes rapidly over half a continent has nearly finished all he can be expected to do; he must soon give place to the surveyor who with plane-table and theodolite will content himself with mapping a section of a single province.[13]

Johnston's remarks anticipated the academic studies of China made in the twentieth century. The first extensive social survey, a survey of Peking, was carried out by Sidney Gamble and J.S. Burgess between 1918 and 1919. They had doubted whether the survey method, already in use in America, could be applied satisfactorily to the study of an oriental city. However, they found 'the Chinese most willing to give us detailed information concerning the various phases of their life'.[14] In the 1920s, John Lossing Buck's survey of the Chinese farm economy raised western research to a high level of thoroughness. For his ambitious study of 2,866 farms he operated with a team of investigators. He claimed that by surveying so many farms he compensated for the disadvantage of there being no written records. The lack of documents proved less important than anticipated, because he found that farmers remembered the details of their previous year's business quite clearly, since each detail was a more or less important part of their daily life.[15]

As observers of China, in terms of experience and knowledge, journalists stand between visitors and those who conduct heavyweight surveys. China has attracted some outstanding journalists: George Morrison, Peter Fleming, Edgar Snow, Theodore White, Jack Belden and James Cameron, to mention just a few. Some of them displayed a remarkable determination to get to the spot where news was being made. This commitment took James Bertram to Sian to report on the kidnapping of Chiang Kai-shek, and Edgar Snow to Yenan to report on Communist activity there. Sometimes it seemed as if the greater the obstacles standing in the way of journalists, the greater was their determination to overcome them. When in 1943 the *Ta Kung Pao*, the most independent Chinese newspaper in Chungking, was suppressed for three days because it had carried a report of the famine in Honan, this 'acted like a barb on the foreign press' and Theodore White and Harrison Forman immediately set out for Honan to find out what was going on.

For journalists, the right to travel and to obtain information freely is of the highest importance. Until 1949 western journalists in China usually were free to travel where they wished. That freedom was withdrawn and in the years leading up to the Cultural Revolution, when only a handful of journalists were based in China, their movements and access to sources of information were restricted. The case of Charles Taylor, the Peking correspondent of the Toronto *Globe and Mail* was typical. He relied heavily on official sources, on the English-language service of the New China News Agency, on the half a dozen Peking newspapers and on the very occasional press conference. He could travel, if he wished, to some parts of China, but vast areas were not accessible to him. On his travels, he was met and guided by an interpreter from the China International Travel Service. Nevertheless he claimed that his observations on these trips allowed him to assess living standards and the quality of daily life.[16]

At the beginning of the twentieth century, the dominant western impression of China was that it was a country which did not change. R.K. Douglas, Professor of Chinese at King's College, London, wrote:

Speaking generally, everything that is modern is ancient, and all that is ancient is modern. With the exception of fashions in trivial matters, nothing has changed in China for many centuries.[17]

Another often repeated stereotype was that the habits of the Chinese were diametrically opposed to those of the West. In the eighteenth and nineteenth centuries this observation was often accompanied by a whimsical list of Chinese 'contrarieties'. By the beginning of the twentieth century such whimsy was less usual, though it could still be encountered, for example in Revd E.J. Hardy's *John Chinaman at Home*. The view which persisted was that there was a great gulf in understanding between Chinese and westerners. The American journalist George Lynch, who went to China to cover the relief of the Peking legations, remarked:

If a section of the population of the planet Mars had been suddenly dumped down on that big tract of country bordering the Gulf of Pechili, their poles of civilisation could not have been more widely separated, their want of comprehension one of the other could hardly have been greater.[18]

Western 'images' of Asia, and of China in particular, have over the years been subject to sharp changes. Harold Isaacs wrote about, 'the shifting of the sets of favorable and unfavorable images that we carry in our heads about other people', and he identified the two poles of the images the West held of the Chinese:

Down through time, from Marco Polo to Mao Tse-tung, the Chinese have appeared to us as superior people and inferior people, outrageous heathen and attractive humanists, wisely benevolent sages and deviously cunning villains, thrifty and honorable men and sly and corrupt cheats, heroically enduring stoics and cruel and sadistic murderers, masses of hardworking persevering people and masses of antlike creatures indifferent to human life, comic opera soldiers and formidable warriors.[19]

This tendency to switch sharply between the two poles of favourable and unfavourable images is illustrated by the contrast between many of the extracts which have been chosen. At the time of the Boxer Rebellion the negative image dominated, but in the late imperial and early republican period a more complicated set of reactions can be observed. A programme of reform was initiated and the term 'Young China' was applied to all those who took the side of reform. This term was greeted by some western writers with approval but by others with derision. Thereafter political partisanship became a reason for the polarization of views. After the establishment of the Chinese Communist Party in 1921 and after the turbulent events of the Nationalist revolution in China between 1925 and 1927, some western writers took up the cause of Chinese Communism. The first of these was Anna Louise Strong, whose political sympathies had been confirmed by a visit she had made to Russia soon after the revolution. Her book, *China's Millions*, was based on her experiences of the Nationalist revolution in China. She wrote passionately about the hopes of the popular movement, and of the counter-revolution which had destroyed any chance of its immediate success. This genre of western writing was continued by Agnes Smedley, Israel Epstein and several others.

After the Communist victory in 1949 and the outbreak of the Korean War, negative impressions were dominant. Because western powers withdrew their diplomats and because most commercial firms and Christian missionaries had been forced to leave, first-hand reports on China through western eyes were rare and the enormous changes which were taking place went unreported. The danger of this ignorance was stressed by the French journalist Robert Guillain, who went back to China in 1955:

> As a mere journalist I found out, as soon as I entered China, that there were great gaps in my knowledge of the country. . . . If I, as a journalist, had cause to regret my ignorance of these transformations, how much more dangerous is it for governments like those of Paris and Washington to allow themselves similar 'gaps' in their knowledge of a country which, today, is one of the most important in the world?[20]

In 1955, at the Bandung Conference, Chou En-lai issued a general invitation to the West to 'come and see' what was happening in China. In the same way that westerners had travelled to the Soviet Union in the 1920s and 1930s, China now became the objective of political pilgrimages. Many of the pilgrims' accounts, based on brief and stereotyped visits, should be treated with caution, although some did admit to the limitations of their experience and the extent to which their impressions had been manipulated.

Suzanne Labin rejected reports from western travellers of this kind and sought information on the 'real' China by interviewing refugees who had arrived in Hong Kong, whose emigration, she claimed, was not that of the dispossessed – their evidence might be coloured by resentment – but was the emigration of ordinary people fleeing from a new order after living under it for a number of years:

> ... It seemed to me unforgivable that no attempt should be made to take advantage of this extraordinary exodus in order to get at the truth. The stories of ordinary people of all trades and occupations who have experienced the conditions of everyday life under the new régime provide us with the most revealing information concerning the nature of the régime – information which is much more significant than the shallow data which is all that the casual visitor can provide.[21]

But to write about China from the security of Hong Kong was liable to expose a writer to criticism. Eric Ranawake once parodied the China Watcher's style:

> It was my practised eye that spotted the missing third button on Chou's tunic, in the photograph showing him greeting the workers' delegation from Rumania. From that I concluded that there was a famine in Cheung Yeun Province. A simple deduction that comes naturally to the experienced China Watcher. You see, all button factories are sited in the Cheung Yeun Province, and if Chou is short of a button, the trained mind jumps to the conclusion – that the button workers are dead from starvation. My report made headlines round the world.[22]

Of the events of modern Chinese history which have provoked conflicting interpretations among western observers, the Cultural Revolution of 1966–9 must stand out as exceptional. Not surprisingly,

Anthony Grey, who was held as a hostage in Peking, portrayed the movement as fanatical. On the other hand Neale Hunter, who remained in Shanghai throughout its first stage, wrote disparagingly about the 'failure of the China-watchers and Sinologists to convey an intelligible explanation of the movement'. This was because they continued to represent nineteenth-century western attitudes to China: 'They looked at China from the outside, instead of endeavoring to see with Chinese eyes.' For Hunter the Cultural Revolution offered 'a perfect chance to get the feel of China':

> . . . It was one of the rare occasions when a whole culture drops its mask, when thousands of people come out and speak their minds. Red Guard wall posters and newspapers revealed more about China and the Chinese in that first year of debate than all the *lettres édifiantes* of the Jesuits, pompous scholarship of the old Sinologists, or jargoned doctoral theses of our day. It was a unique opportunity to listen and learn.[23]

In the 1970s, in the post-Cultural Revolution period, many changes believed to be occurring in Chinese society were eulogized by western writers. Some found in China a new model for the West, some even went so far as to alter their lifestyle to approach that of the Chinese – for example Ruth Sidel, an American sociologist noted, 'Rather than feeling oppressed by the similarity of Chinese clothing, I soon felt overdressed and began myself not to wear jewelry.'[24]

The most admired aspect of these changes was the extent to which rural China appeared to have responded to the challenges of poverty and population growth and to present a shining exception to the destitution of the Third World. This view was challenged by Stephen Mosher, an American research student, who carried out fieldwork in Kwangtung province. He included in his book *Broken Earth* a graphic description of the late termination of abortions. He was denounced in China and in the United States – and was expelled from Stanford University – for having taken and published, without her permission, the photograph of a woman undergoing an abortion. In the preface to *Broken Earth*, Mosher insisted that his real offence was that he had unmasked the truth about rural China, which was that the peasants were not better off under Communism.[25]

Subsequently, several writers admitted openly that their views of the Cultural Revolution had changed. At that time, Claudie Broyelle had convinced herself that the reason why late marriage was promoted in China was not for population control, but as 'a measure aimed at the emancipation of women'. She later admitted, 'It was the purest day-dream on my part, which the smallest acquaintance with life in China saw collapse like a house of cards.'[26]

This disillusionment with China as a model for emulation was gradually balanced by a more positive view of China as a tourist destination. The lack of political freedom was deplored, but signs of economic progress were welcomed. Any survey of western perceptions of China would have predicted that such a positive view would not last for long. The tragic events of 4 June 1989 gave rise to further adverse comments and ensured that this selection of views would conclude on a sombre note.

In a brief anthology it is not possible to do more than provide samples of the material which is available in these sources. As wide a variety of opinions as possible has been included, even opinions which, because of their racist character, may be regarded as deplorable. Inevitably the selection is subjective and many books which merit being included have been omitted for reasons of space. The extracts are presented in a chronological order and the introductory section to each chapter briefly explains the context and origin of the passages used.

NOTES

1. Anna Louise Strong, *China's Millions*, London, 1936, p. 163.
2. Nym Wales, ed., *Red Dust: Autobiographies of Chinese Communists*, Stanford, 1952, p. ix.
3. A. Winnington, *The Slaves of the Cool Mountains*, London, 1959, author's note.
4. Quoted by Dick Wilson in the Introduction to Otto Braun, *A Comintern Agent in China 1932–1939*, London, 1982, p. viii.
5. W.A. Cornaby, *China Under the Search-Light*, London, 1901, pp. 3–4.
6. W.R. Geddes, *Peasant Life in Communist China*, New York, 1963, pp. 1–8.

7. Peter Fleming, *One's Company*, London, 1934.
8. Simone de Beauvoir, *The Long March*, London, 1958, p. 19.
9. E. Dingle, *Across China on Foot*, Bristol, 1911, p. viii.
10. Sven Lindqvist, *China in Crisis*, London, 1965, pp. 99, 101.
11. E.A. Ross, *The Changing Chinese*, London, 1911, pp. xv–xvi.
12. Karl A. Wittfogel, Preface to Olga Lang, *Chinese Family and Society*, n.p., 1946, 1968, p. vii.
13. R.F. Johnston, *Lion and Dragon in Northern China*, New York, 1910, p. 4.
14. Sidney D. Gamble and John Stewart Burgess, *Peking: A Social Survey*, New York, 1921, pp. xiii–xiv.
15. J.L. Buck, *Chinese Farm Economy*, Chicago, 1930, pp. 1–4.
16. Charles Taylor, *Reporter in Red China*, London, 1967, pp. 3–29.
17. R.K. Douglas, *Society in China*, London, 1895, p. 1.
18. G. Lynch, *The War of the Civilisations*, London, 1901, p. x.
19. Harold R. Isaacs, *Images of Asia: American Views of China and India*, New York, 1972, p. xi.
20. R. Guillain, *The Blue Ants: 600 Million Chinese under the Red Flag*, London, 1957, p. viii.
21. Suzanne Labin, *The Anthill*, London, 1960, p. ix.
22. Eric Ranawake, 'The Oriental Syndrome, by a China Watching Pro', *The Asian*, 10 October 1971, quoted in Peter Harris, *Political China Observed*, London, 1980, p. 23.
23. Neale Hunter, *Shanghai Journal*, London, 1969, pp. 6–7.
24. Ruth Sidel, *Women and Child Care in China*, Harmondsworth, 1972, revised edition 1982, p. 42.
25. C. Mackerras, *Western Images of China*, Hong Kong, 1989, p. 238.
26. Claudie Broyelle et al., *China: A Second Look*, Brighton, 1980, p. 8.

THE BOXER UPRISING AND LATE IMPERIAL REFORMS

At the beginning of the twentieth century many westerners held a negative view of the Chinese, but few were as hostile as Eliza Scidmore, an American tourist and professional writer, who compared them with the Japanese. She disparaged China as a destination for the tourist, commenting that, 'Neither Murray nor Baedeker has penetrated the empire – they have no need to; none calls them' (1).

In 1900 the Boxer Uprising swept China and culminated in the siege of the foreign legations in Peking. More than 150 eyewitness descriptions were published in European languages. One of the best-informed accounts was by the American Board missionary A.H. Smith (2). Another missionary, Revd Archibald Glover of the China Inland Mission lived at Lu-an, about 350 miles south-west of Peking. In June 1900, in the face of growing anti-foreign agitation, he, his pregnant wife, their two children and a companion left their station and began a desperate journey which eventually took them to Hankow. They suffered numerous assaults, were sentenced to death and suffered such privations that the companion and one of the children died (3).

Other accounts described the siege of Peking. Lancelot Giles, the son of Herbert Giles, the Professor of Chinese at Cambridge University, kept a diary of the siege to provide his father with an accurate version of events. However, Professor Giles refused to believe that the Chinese were capable of such barbaric behaviour (4 and 5). After the relief of the legations came the allied sack of Peking. B.L. Putnam Weale, a pseudonym for B.L. Simpson, was among those who witnessed what occurred. He wandered into the Imperial Palace and even went into the Empress Dowager's bedroom (6). George Lynch noted the eagerness with which westerners looted (7). It appeared that after these disastrous events, China would be partitioned, but Sir Robert Hart, the head of the Imperial Maritime Customs, correctly anticipated what was to be the future policy of the allies, namely to continue to do business as usual with the Chinese government (8).

A year later, J.O.P. Bland and E. Backhouse recorded the return of the Empress Dowager to Peking (9). At the time of the Uprising, she had ordered the extermination of foreigners, but after its suppression she concluded that the Manchus' best chance of survival lay in promoting reform and adopting a friendly attitude to westerners, a change of mind which Mrs Conger, the wife of the American minister accepted eagerly (10). This new friendliness gave westerners unprecedented access to the court. Katharine Carl, an American artist, spent nine months there. In her account of court life she described the Chief Eunuch, Li Lien-ying, whom scandal associated improperly with the Empress Dowager (11). Another privileged observer was Willard Straight, a student-interpreter with the Imperial Maritime Customs. In 1903 he disguised himself as a monk and secretly watched the emperor perform a ceremony at a Buddhist temple near Peking (12). Straight also illustrated a light work by J.O.P. Bland, one of the best-known figures on the China coast. Bland's description of shooting pheasants and bamboo partridge in the Yangtze estuary contained patronizing comments on the accidental shooting of Chinese peasants (13). A similar tone was adopted by the Revd E.J. Hardy, chaplain to the British forces in China, when writing on the subject of Chinese food (14).

In the last years of the Empire, western encroachment on China continued apace. France acquired a sphere of influence in the south-west to complement her colonial possessions in Indo-China. It was from there that Vicomte d'Ollone, a major in the French army, launched an expedition to contact minority groups in the area (15). China's political weakness also allowed other forms of encroachment: for example the appropriation of archaeological treasures in Chinese Central Asia. The most dramatic discovery was that of the hidden library of Tun-huang, located by Aurel Stein in 1907 (16).

In its last years the Manchu dynasty sought to survive through endorsing a programme of reform. Dr W.A.P. Martin, former President of the Chinese Imperial University, noted the change in Chinese attitudes to technology (17). Edward Ross, an American Professor of Sociology, although convinced that racial weaknesses would always handicap the Chinese attempts at reform, praised the success of the anti-opium campaign in Foochow, which had been launched in 1906, after the Empress Dowager had commanded that the growth, sale and consumption of opium should cease within ten years (18). The campaign against the growing of the opium poppy was the subject of a remarkably thorough investigation by Sir Alexander Hosie, a former British diplomatic officer (19). Margaret Burton, on a six-month trip to China, investigated the education of women, especially in mission schools, and she too found much to enthuse about (20). Henri Borel, a correspondent of the Amsterdam *Telegraaf,* was struck by the progress of reform in Peking. He believed that there could be no rapid transition from the tyranny of the imperial system to parliamentary government, but was convinced of the sincerity of some Chinese pursuing that aim (21). George Morrison, *The Times* correspondent in China, took issue with J.O.P. Bland on the subject of the prospects of constitutional reform in China. He wrote to Valentine Chirol, head of the newspaper's foreign department, expressing high hopes of the new provincial assemblies (22).

However, much remained unchanged. Edwin Dingle, a journalist, who walked from western China to Burma between 1909 and 1910, noted the unaltered character of the province of Yünnan (23). Archibald Little described the lack of response to the introduction of the telegraph to Hupei province (24), and Reginald Johnston, the District Officer of the British territory of Weihaiwei in Shantung, stressed the survival of tradition in the area despite fifteen years' contact with western civilization (25).

1) *Their very numbers and sameness appal one*
(Eliza R. Scidmore, *China: The Long-Lived Empire*, pp. 4–6)
No Occidental ever saw within or understood the working of the yellow brain, which starts from and arrives at a different point by reverse and inverse processes we can neither follow nor comprehend. . . . Of all Orientals, no race is so alien. Not a memory nor a custom, not a tradition nor an idea, not a root-word nor a symbol of any kind associates our past with their past. There is little sympathy, no kinship

nor common feeling, and never affection possible between the Anglo-Saxon and the Chinese. . . .

Their very numbers and sameness appal one, the frightful likeness of any one individual to all the other three hundred odd millions of his own people. Everywhere, from end to end of the vast empire, one finds them cast in the same unvarying physical and mental mold – the same yellow skin, hard features, and harsh, mechanical voice; the same houses, graves, and clothes; the same prejudices, superstitions, and customs; the same selfish conservatism, blind worship of precedent and antiquity; a monotony, unanimity, and repetition of life, character, and incident, that offend one almost to resentment. Everywhere on their tenth of the globe, from the edge of Siberia to the end of Cochin China, the same ignoble queue and the senseless cotton shoe are worn; everywhere this fifth of the human race is sunk in dirt and disorder, decadent, degenerate, indifferent to a fallen estate, consumed with conceit, selfish, vain, cowardly, and superstitious, without imagination, sentiment, chivalry, or sense of humor, combating with most zeal anything that would alter conditions even for the better, indifferent as to who rules or usurps the throne.

2) *The 'Red Lantern Light' society*
(A.H. Smith, *China in Convulsion*, II, p. 662)

Among the many singular phenomena connected with the rise and spread of the Boxer sect, nothing seems stranger or more in defiance of Chinese customs and the ideals of long generations than the accompanying organization of the 'Hung Têng Chou' or 'Red Lantern Light' society. This was composed of young girls between the ages of ten and twenty, just the age when Chinese maidens are most carefully hidden in the seclusion of their homes. . . .

These girls in large companies were taken to the temples, put under the low and vicious men who were the Boxer leaders, and after a certain amount of drill accompanied Boxer bands in their public parades. Their uniform was entirely of red, red cloth about their heads, red shoes on their feet, red banners in their hands. Their training was similar to that given Boxer boys, the repetition of charms by the leader, who was sometimes a man, sometimes a woman, – following this the hypnotic trance, then a frenzy of desire to fight with sword or spear or gun.

The special power said to belong to these girls was to ride upon the clouds and to point out the houses of foreigners or their friends, Christians or others. From the clouds they could kindle a fire that would harm none but those proscribed. From the clouds, too, they could cause the iron battle-ships of the enemy to burn like tinder.

3) *The breaking of the storm*
(A.E. Glover, *A Thousand Miles of Miracle in China*, pp. 48–50)

All was quiet as we entered the inn yard, and we began to prepare the children's food. The meal was not ready before the yard was filled with a pushing, curious crowd. It was no use to plead the heat of the day and the fatigue of travel. Every view point was occupied. The rice paper was torn from the window of the small guest-room and every aperture framed a face.

This in itself would not have troubled us much. But with riot in the air we knew not what might lie behind. We had scarcely swallowed a bowl of food when Chi-fah came in and said, 'We must be off at once, or I cannot answer for the consequences.' As quickly as might be, but without betraying undue haste, we settled ourselves once more in our litters, almost unfed and wholly unrested. The crowd had now grown to immense proportions. The whole of that large village town seemed to be there thronging about us, following behind as we moved out of the inn yard and closely pressing us to the gate with an ominous silence. Suddenly, as we cleared the gate, a yell went up, 'Foreign devils! kill them!' and a storm of stones and hard clay clods rained about the litters. A large stone caught my little boy full in the chest and knocked him flat. The dear little fellow cried bitterly, but he soon recovered, as I prayed with him and told him not to be afraid because God was with us. Several stones entered the litter, but I parried them with a pillow. The mules were hit and became very restive, so that I thought we should be turned over; but by shifting now to one side now to the other, I contrived to maintain the balance of the litter.

The framework now began to show signs of giving way under the shower of missiles. It would have been broken up ere this but for the unusual fact that the covering was formed of new straw mats over which, as a protection against the intense heat, we had thrown a thick cotton wool coverlet. The coverlets were torn off and the stones showered against the yielding straw.

Just as the mats were parting the litters were surrounded and the stoning all but ceased. A big, powerful man seized the mule's head, and looking in at me ordered me to get out. I asked him what he wanted with me, and he said, 'I have something to say to you; get down at once.' Knowing well enough that once down I should never get up again I refused, and said, 'If my respected elder brother wishes to say anything, I can listen to him just as well inside as out.'

'You are Roman Catholics,' he said; 'get down, I tell you.'

'We are nothing of the sort; we abhor the Roman Catholic religion.'

'Not Roman Catholics! what are you then?'

'Our religion is the true religion of Jesus, and our doctrine the pure doctrine of God.'

The man turned to the crowd and said, 'They are not T'ien Chu Kiao' (Roman Catholics), 'they are Ie-su Kiao' (Protestants). 'Let them go on.'

4) *The destruction of the Han-lin Library*
(L. Giles, *The Siege of the Peking Legations*, p. 126)

At 11.15 a.m. a fire was reported in the Hanlin, where the Chinese were entrenched. It was got under, and the Hanlin cleared of Chinese troops.

There was some doubt as to whether we should occupy the Hanlin as a strategic position, and pull down the buildings as a preventive of fires. It was argued, however, that the Chinese would never set fire to so venerable a monument of the country's literature.

This was set at naught by the Chinese setting fire to the various buildings all through the day. The Library was almost entirely destroyed; an attempt was made to save the famous *Yung lu ta tien* but heaps of volumes had been destroyed, so the attempt was given up. I secured volume 13,345 (!!) for myself, merely as a specimen. The pages are one foot by one foot eight inches and the volumes vary from half an inch to one inch in thickness. Each page has eight columns, each column contains two rows of twenty-six characters.

I also picked up a couple of the essays written by some candidate for one of the great examinations.

Within the next few days we completed the work begun by the Chinese and razed the Hanlin to the ground.

5) *Treatment of Boxer prisoners*
(L. Giles, *The Siege of the Peking Legations*, pp. 113, 120, 129)
June 14th
At 12.45 p.m. Captain Wray (Royal Marines), being on duty at the North Bridge, captured a Boxer who was calmly strolling across. He appeared in a half-dazed and mesmerized condition, and was un-armed, or else he would have been shot on the spot. He wore a yellow girdle and had a square piece of red flannel on his chest, hung from his neck. This is supposed to render all Boxers absolutely invulnerable. He was put in the cells, awaiting a decision as to his fate. Several of the Chinese servants forthwith left the Legation for good, saying that this Boxer would breathe fire and burn the place about our ears! [. . .]
June 19th
   Meanwhile another man had been walking over the bridge, when this same sergeant caught sight of about an inch of red cloth beneath his jacket. This man too was seized, and found to be garbed in full Boxer uniform. [. . .]
June 25th
   6.30 a.m. Our two Boxer prisoners, (see above), were shot, and their bodies chucked over the wall.

6) *In the Empress's bedroom*
(B.L. Putnam Weale, *Indiscreet Letters from Peking*, pp. 268–9)
At last we were in this dear Empress's bedroom, the abode which shelters for such a considerable number of hours of every twenty-four the most powerful woman in Asia. We looked eagerly. At one side of the room was a large bed, beautifully adorned with embroidered hangings; ranged round there was a profusion of handsome carved-wood furniture, with European chairs upholstered in a style out of keeping with the rest; on a high stand there were jewelled clocks noisily ticking; and hidden modestly in one corner was nothing less than a magnificent silver *pot de chambre*. She was here evidently very much at her ease, the dear old lady. That little detail delighted me. The rest was rather *banal*.
   Sans cérémonie, I seated myself on the Imperial bed – it seemed to be the most peaceful act of vandalism I could commit in repayment for certain discomforts occasioned by this old lady's whims during eight weeks of rifle-fire. And as my recollections went back to those terrible

days, I came down heavily as I could on this august couch. I must confess that as a bed it was excellent; the old lady must have slept well through it all, whilst she caused us our ceaseless vigil. . . .

This solitude in the most secluded of spots in the whole Palace made us more and more inquisitive, and soon K – and myself were hard at work, rummaging every likely hiding-place.

7) *Looting in Peking*
(G. Lynch, *The War of the Civilisations*, pp. 184–5)
Pearls are easily portable things, and of these precious jewels with the Chinese there must have been an enormous quantity in Pekin, but not a very great number were found by the soldiers. I saw some beautiful watches set with pearls however. Watches were in great profusion amongst the soldiers.

Passing through Tung-Chow, a Russian soldier was to be seen who had possessed himself of a big box full of watches. He could literally dive his arm right up to the elbow in them. One dollar each he was selling them at.

In the Russian camp at the base of Coal Hill the men were to be seen drinking out of porcelain and jade bowls. An officer in the Welsh regiment passing one day saw a Russian drinking at a well from a magnificently carved green jade goblet. 'How much?' The Russian held up one finger, meaning one dollar, equal to two shillings, and the deal took place to the satisfaction of both.

8) *The awakening of China*
(Sir Robert Hart, "*These from the Land of Sinim*", pp. 49–50)
This episode of to-day is not meaningless – it is the prelude to a century of change and the keynote of the future history of the Far East: the China of the year 2000 will be very different from the China of 1900! National sentiment is a constant factor which must be recognized, and not eliminated, when dealing with national facts, and the one feeling that is universal in China is pride in Chinese institutions and contempt for foreign: treaty intercourse has not altered this – if anything, it has deepened it, and the future will not be uninfluenced by it. The first question now to be settled by the Treaty Powers is how to make peace, for China is at war with all; and what conditions to impose to safeguard the future, for the stipulations of the past have been set at

defiance and obliterated. There would seem to be a choice between three courses – partition, change of dynasty, or patching up the Manchoo rule. As regards partition – that plan, like every other, has its good and its bad sides; but, with such an enormous population, it could never be expected to be a final settlement. . . . That the future will have a 'yellow' question – perhaps a yellow 'peril' – to deal with, is as certain as that the sun will shine tomorrow. . . . As to setting up a new dynasty – there is no man of mark all China would accept; the plan would plunge the country into years of anarchy. . . . Remains, then, the third plan – to accept the existing dynasty as a going concern, and, in a word, make the best of it.

9) *The return of the Empress Dowager to Peking*
(J.O.P. Bland and E. Backhouse, *China under the Empress Dowager*, pp. 401–2)

At noon on the 6th of January, 1902, the Imperial party arrived by special train at the temporary station which had been erected close to the Southern walls of Peking. . . . Large pavilions, handsomely decorated, had been erected near the station, in which the Old Buddha and the Emperor were to be received; they were furnished with a throne of gold lacquer, cloisonné altar vessels and many valuable pieces of porcelain. Several hundreds of the highest metropolitan officials were in attendance, and a special place had been provided for foreigners. As the long train of over thirty carriages drew up at the station, the keen face of the Old Buddha was seen anxiously scanning her surroundings from one of the windows of her car. With her were the young Empress and the Princess Imperial, while the chief eunuch, Li Lien-ying, was in attendance. Recognising Her Majesty, every official fell upon his knees, whilst Chi Lu, chief officer of the Household, officiously shouted to the foreigners to remove their hats (which they had already done). The first to emerge from the train was the chief eunuch, who proceeded forthwith to check the long list of provincial tribute and treasure, mountainous loads of baggage which had travelled with the Court from the start and under Her Majesty's close personal supervision. After the eunuch came the Emperor, evidently extremely nervous, who, at a sign from Her Majesty, hurried into his sedan-chair and was swiftly borne away, without a word or a sign of recognition to any of the officials in attendance. After his departure, the Empress came out and stood upon the platform at the end of her carriage. 'Quite a number of foreigners are here, I see,' she was heard to observe. She saluted them in accordance with the etiquette observed by Chinese women – bowing and raising her crossed hands. . . . She stood there for some five minutes in full view of the crowd, talking energetically with the bystanders, and looking extremely well and youthful for her age, until the chief eunuch returned and handed her the list of baggage and treasure, which she scanned with close attention and then returned to him with an expression of satisfaction.

10) *An audience at court, 1902*
(Sarah Pike Conger, *Letters from China*, pp. 217–22)
On February first, the Emperor and the Empress Dowager received the ladies of the Diplomatic Corps, the wives of the Commanders of the Legation Guards, and the children, in an audience. A wonderful day it was! [. . .]

At the door of the throne room we halted, fell into our rightful places, and entered, bowing three times at intervals as we approached the throne of Her Majesty. She sat back of a long table, upon which lay a beautiful coral sceptre. As we approached, the Empress Dowager smiled a recognition to me, as I was the only one of the group of ladies she had met before. As the Dean of the ladies of the Diplomatic Corps, I addressed Her Majesty. . . .

'Your Majesty, the ladies of the Diplomatic Corps have responded with pleasure to your kind invitation for this audience; and we most heartily congratulate you and all the Imperial Court that the unfortunate situation which led you to abandon your beautiful capital has been so happily resolved. . . .

The events of the past two years must be as painful to you as they are to the rest of the world; but the sting of the sad experience may be eliminated . . . through the establishment of better, franker, more trustful, and friendlier relations between China and the other peoples of the earth. . . .

The recent Imperial Edicts give promise of great good to your people and to your vast Empire, and it is our earnest prayer that God may preserve Your Majesty and the Emperor and guide you to the fullest fruition of this promise.'

When I finished reading, Prince Ch'ing stepped upon the throne and, kneeling to the Empress Dowager, took from her hand her reply. Then followed the presentation of the ladies and children according to rank. . . . After these presentations we were escorted to another large room, where an informal reception was held. The Empress Dowager was there and as we entered she asked for 'Kang Tai Tai' – my Chinese name – and I was presented to her. She took my hands in both of hers, and her feelings overcame her. When she was able to control her voice, she said, 'I regret, and grieve over the late troubles. It was a grave mistake, and China will hereafter be a friend to foreigners. No such affair will again happen. China will protect the foreigner, and we hope to be friends in the future.'

'We believe that you are sincere,' I replied. 'By knowing each other better we believe we shall become friends.'

The Empress Dowager then asked if there were any other ladies present who were in the siege. Mrs. Bainbridge of the American Legation and Mrs. Saussine of the French Legation were presented. She again turned to me, extending both hands, and took mine with a few uninterpreted Chinese words. And then taking from one of her fingers a heavy, carved gold ring set with an elegant pearl, she placed it upon one of mine; then from her wrists she took choice bracelets and placed them upon my wrists. To each lady she presented gifts of great value. The children and the interpreters were also kindly remembered.

From here we were escorted to the banquet hall, where three long tables were spread with the choicest Chinese food. We were asked to be seated. A vacant chair was at the end of the table, at my left. As the Empress Dowager entered we all arose. She came to this vacant chair, took her glass of wine, and we did likewise. She placed her glass in my left hand, gracefully pressed my two hands together, so that the glasses touched, and said, 'United.' She then took my glass, leaving me hers, and raised the glass to all, and all responded. Then cups of tea were served. The Empress Dowager took one with both hands and placing it in mine, lifted it to my lips. After all were served with tea, we were invited to be seated. The Empress Dowager then took a filled biscuit, broke it, and placed a small piece of it in my mouth. She paid like compliments to other ministers' wives, and placed a morsel upon the plates of other guests at the same table. [. . .]

There were sharp and bitter criticisms of the ladies' acceptance of the Imperial invitation. Individual bitterness still has its poison and would keep the breach open and even widen it if possible; but national wisdom, through peace negotiations, seeks to close the breach. Pressing the thorns of sorrow and revenge deeper into our hearts will never lessen the sting of the horrible past nor permit us to rest in peace.

11) *Her Majesty's Chief Eunuchs*
(Katherine Carl, *With the Empress Dowager of China*, pp. 124–6)
Her Majesty's Chief Eunuch has almost the power in Peking, among officials and courtiers, that 'Son Eminence Grise' had at the Court of Louis XIII of France. He is courted and fawned upon, receives magnificent presents, and nobles of high degree wait upon his pleasure; but while he occupies this high position with outsiders, in the Palace I saw no evidence of his having any unusual power with Her Majesty. . . . [. . .]

In person he is tall and thin. His head is, in type, like Savonarola's. He has a Roman nose, a massive lean jaw, a protruding lower lip, and very shrewd eyes, full of intelligence, that shine out of sunken orbits. His face is much wrinkled and his skin like old parchment. Though only sixty years old, he looks seventy-five, and is the oldest eunuch in the Palace. He has been there since the age of ten. He has elegant, insinuating manners, speaks excellent Chinese – having a fine enunciation, a good choice of words, and a low, pleasant voice. If one may judge from appearances, he possesses ability in a marked degree. [. . .]

Her Majesty's second eunuch, Sui, who is of equal rank with Li Lien Ying, is as unlike him as two people could possibly be, both as to person, character, mental and moral nature. This one has none of the qualities of the intriguer – no Macchiavellian schemes would be forwarded by him. He is almost a giant in size, tall and heavy. He is forty-six years old, and has a round, full face, without a line – a typical Chinese face, as we know it from pictures, benevolent and kind. He, also, is a good Chinese scholar, and, of course, speaks it elegantly. Her Majesty will have no one around her person who does not speak it well. If it be true that Her Majesty, in choosing her ministers, tries to have them the opposites of each other, so that she may thus hear the different sides of a question and arrive at more just conclusions, her two Chief Eunuchs seem to have been chosen in the same way.

12) *The Emperor after performing a Buddhist ceremony*
(H. Croly, *Willard Straight*, pp. 108–9)
At last there was a stir, and all eyes were turned to the east. The High
Priest kneeled and the idlers rose to their feet in expectancy. At a
rapid pace the same little official came forward, followed by the priests
with the censors, then several more officials and finally the Emperor
himself. In the first instance it had been impossible to distinguish him
save by the fact of his wearing the round dragon badge on his
breast. . . . As he came forward at a rapid but withal dignified pace, he
made a peculiar impression. He wore simply the ordinary official hat
with the blood-red button, a dark silken surcoat hid even his dragon
insignia, and one could scarcely realize that this very young, very
delicate looking man was the ruler in name at least of four hundred
million people. A weak face, with arching, jet-black eyebrows, his eyes
on the ground before him, his shoulders and head thrown back,
marching with a fixed pace steadily forward. He passed to the left of
his chair and then went quietly in, the chair bearers kneeling as he did
so, and officials kneeling and standing on either side. Without a word,
without any delay, the chair was raised, the bodyguard fell in to the
rear and followed by a stand of Imperial yellow banners with ermine
streamers, the cortège passed through the side gate most unpreten-
tiously, and as they left the bugles sounded and the whole procession
moved on. It was wonderful, the precision, the quiet with which all
was done, and the uproar which followed his departure.

13) *Rough shooting in the Yangtze delta*
(J.O.P. Bland, *Houseboat Days in China*, pp. 61–3)
But there is one animal which none of us willingly shoots, yet which,
sooner or later, figures in every bag – *Homo sinensis* to wit, our Chinese
fellow man. When one remembers how ubiquitous and numerous is
this blue clad creature, how its innate curiosity and other forms of
cussedness invite disaster, the only wonder is that we bag so few.
Suddenly rising between you and a flushed quail in the cotton, or
bobbing up from behind a grave, as you are snapping at a partridge –
how often have we seen his sheepish grin as the gun comes away just in
time, that grin which broadens as the marrow trickles in our bones, and
we curse him in the ecstasy of our relief? But every pitcher has its
appointed day, and most of us, either for our own or for another's

offences, have heard the *vox humana* rise strident from cover and seen our undesired 'bag' emerge, loudly bemoaning his (or her) impending doom. If it be a man, reason and sycee salve will often adjust matters unless the wounds are serious; but if your quarry is an old woman, or if one of these shrill viragos appear screaming on the scene, your best plan is to make swiftly for the boat, and from that coign of vantage discuss matters through the lowdah. Like everything else in China the cost of peppering a native has increased absurdly of recent years, and for those who do not speak the language it has become almost prohibitive in some of the more turbulent districts. We all remember the days when a dollar and a bit of sticking plaster would atone for half a charge of No. 6; now a dollar a pellet is cheap enough as prices go, and the nearer you are to schools of Western learning and the unspeakable Baboo, the higher the value of a native's injured feelings . . . . This fly lurking in the amber of our up-country joys is one of the inevitable results of our civilising theories about the rights of man; happily it comes but rarely to the surface. And, after all, this is the Chinaman's country through which we stride so blithe and *débonnaire* with beaters, dogs, and guns, and if we have to pay occasionally for our bad luck or his stupidity, why, let us pay cheerfully, and thank Heaven he is still unsophisticated or good-natured enough to dispense with barbed-wire fences and the laws of trespass.

14) *Chinese food*
(Revd E.J. Hardy, *John Chinaman at Home*, pp. 108–9)
A caldron worthy of the witches in 'Macbeth' could be filled by a few Chinese hucksters. One could contribute eye of newt, and toe of frog, another several kinds of lizards, a third black-beetles and grasshoppers. In a barrel are what look like dried prunes. 'What are those?' you ask a grinning Chinaman. Popping one into his mouth, he answers, 'That belong cocky-loachee. Velly good.' They are dried cockroaches!

A coolie picks up from a street stall with a wire fork provided for the purpose and eats a piece of candied ginger, of lotus-root, of melon, and of everything in the collection. For each tit-bit he pays a cash or about the fortieth part of a penny. Imagine a British workman doing anything so innocent as eat sweets at a street stall! [. . .]

. . . The Chinese are nearly as fond of pickles as are British soldiers – pickled nuts, pickled cabbage, pickled onions, and they like fruits when both salted and sugared. With soy sauce anything will go down. Earthworms when fried crisp are relished, and so are silkworms when they have done their work and nothing more can be got out of them. Locusts are thought to have a better flavour and to be more nutritious if they are thrown into boiling oil when alive.

Foreigners used to classify the beef obtainable in Peking as 'horse,' 'camel,' 'donkey,' or 'precipice.' The last was that of a beast that had been killed by a fall. . . .

To eat venison is to incur the danger of becoming as timid as deer. Pork, which is eaten everywhere in China, is often dishonestly treated. Its weight is added to by being injected with water, the point of the syringe being passed into a large vein. In this way the Chinese water their stock when dead!

15) *An extraordinary exhibition of skill*
(Vicomte d'Ollone, *In Forbidden China*, pp. 80–1)
On the following morning our friend Shuka, followed by his notables, entered our house and invited us to come and see some equestrian exercises; he led us in a troop to the other side of the river, into Ashu territory. We there found our friend Sia-Moudjei and a considerable crowd of people gathered before a vast circular race-course, evidently much frequented; and we were surprised to learn what we afterwards saw for ourselves, that in the outskirts of almost all the villages there were similar enclosures, where the young horsemen exercised the noble art of equitation.

Then began the most astonishing acrobatic feats. Several young men galloped at high speed into the circular enclosure, where they threw themselves back until the head was almost touching the crupper; but instead of keeping the legs down, as would be done in Europe, they lifted them right up, thus combining the two exercises known in French equitation as 'Flexion of the loins backwards' and 'Elevation of the thighs.' They had, of course, no grip of their mounts whatever, and kept on the backs of their animals only by the exercise of the most extraordinary suppleness, which enabled them to keep their equilibrium at a giddy pace, as though their bodies were one with their horses. The great mantles, held only by a running string round the neck, and streaming backwards with the wind of their flight, prolonged the outline of each horse by at least three or four feet, so that it seemed an apocalyptic monstrosity. The riders made several circuits of the course, giving an extraordinary exhibition of skill.

16) *The hidden library of Tun-huang*
(M. Aurel Stein, *Ruins of Desert Cathay*, II, pp. 171–2)
All doubt, however, disappeared in the end. Late at night Chiang groped his way to my tent in silent elation with a bundle of Chinese rolls which Wang Tao-shih had just brought him in secret, carefully hidden under his flowing black robe, as the first of the promised 'specimens.' The rolls looked unmistakably old as regards writing and paper, and probably contained Buddhist canonical texts; but Chiang needed time to make sure of their character. Next morning he turned up by daybreak, and with a face expressing both triumph and amazement, reported that these fine rolls of paper contained Chinese versions of certain 'Sutras' from the Buddhist canon which the colophons declared to have been brought from India and translated by Hsüan-tsang himself. . . .

. . . Chiang-ssû-yeh realized at once that this discovery was bound to impress the credulous priest as a special interposition on my behalf of the great traveller of sacred memory. So he hastened away to carry the news to the Tao-shih . . . to renew his pleading for free access to the hidden manuscript store. The effect was most striking. Before long Chiang returned to report that the portent could be trusted to work its spell. Some hours later he found the wall blocking the entrance to the recess of the temple removed, and on its door being opened by the priest, caught a glimpse of a room crammed full to the roof with manuscript bundles. I had purposely kept away from the Tao-shih's temple all the forenoon, but on getting this news I could no longer restrain my impatience to see the great hoard myself. The day was cloudless and hot, and the 'soldiers' who had followed me about during the morning with my cameras, were now taking their siesta in sound sleep soothed by a good smoke of opium. So accompanied only by Chiang I went to the temple.

I found the priest there evidently still combating his scruples and nervous apprehensions. But under the influence of that quasi-divine hint he now summoned up courage to open before me the rough door closing the narrow entrance which led from the side of the broad front passage into the rock-carved recess, on a level of about four feet above the floor of the former. The sight of the small room disclosed was one to make my eyes open wide. Heaped up in layers, but without any order, there appeared in the dim light of the priest's little lamp a solid mass of manuscript bundles rising to a height of nearly ten feet, and filling, as subsequent measurement showed, close on 500 cubic feet.

17) *The advent of the telegraph*
(W.A.P. Martin, *The Awakening of China*, pp. 204–5)
The advent of railways has been slow in comparison with the telegraph. The provinces are covered with wires. Governors and captains consult with each other by wire, in preference to a tardy exchange of written correspondence. The people, too, appreciate the advantage of communicating by a flash with distant members of their families and of settling questions of business at remote places without stirring from their own doors. To have their thunder god bottled up and brought down to be their courier was to them the wonder of wonders; yet they have now become so accustomed to this startling innovation, that they cease to marvel.

The wireless telegraph is also at work – a little manual, translated by a native Christian, tells people how to use it.

Over forty years ago, when I exhibited the Morse system to the astonished dignitaries of Peking, those old men, though heads of departments, chuckled like children when, touching a button, they heard a bell ring; or when wrapping a wire round their bodies, they saw the lightning leap from point to point. 'It's wonderful,' they exclaimed, 'but we can't use it in our country. The people would steal the wires.' Electric bells are now common appliances in the houses of Chinese who live in foreign settlements. Electric trolleys are soon to be running at Shanghai and Tientsin. Telephones, both private and public, are a convenience much appreciated. Accustomed as the Chinese are to the instantaneous transmission of thought and speech, they have yet to see the *telodyne* – electricity as a transmitter of force. But will they not see it when the trolleys run? The advent of electric power will mark an epoch.

18) *The grapple with the opium evil*
(E.A. Ross, *The Changing Chinese*, pp. 162–5)
Foochow, long a seat of missionary influence, has made the most spectacular fight on opium. When I was there no one under penalty of

confiscation of his goods might smoke opium without registering and taking out a permit. Such a permit is issued only to one who can prove that he has the opium-smoking habit. The number of his permit is posted outside the house where he may smoke and he must not smoke anywhere else. While he is smoking no one may visit him on any pretext, and after he is through all his paraphernalia – pipe, bowl, lamp, opium box, needle, etc., – must be gathered up and put away. . . .

Opium may be sold only by licensed dealers who account for and pay a tax on every ounce they sell, and it may not be sold in the place where it is smoked. No one may cook his opium himself; he must buy it prepared. The amount the registered smoker may buy daily is stated in his permit. . . . The smoker must renew his permit every three months and each time it must be filled out for a less amount. . . .

Under the leadership of Lin, grandson of the famous Imperial Commissioner who destroyed the Indian opium, numerous anti-opium societies sprang into existence. . . . The societies collect and break up paraphernalia seized in their raids or given up by reformed smokers. From time to time the stock on hand is stacked up in a public place and solemnly burned to signalize the progress of the campaign. Eleven burnings have taken place and the pipes, bowls, plates, lamps, and opium boxes sacrificed by fire are upwards of twenty-five thousand. Nothing is spared and no curio seeker need hope to rescue some rare and beautiful pipe by a tempting bid.

Thanks to these various endeavors the amount of opium sold in Foochow has fallen off four-fifths and the number of opium-smoking permits out now is less than half the number originally issued. Hardly any but low-class people smoke. . . .

Perhaps no city matches Foochow in the cleverness of its campaign. In many places the effort was made to close the shops and dens at a single sweep. But always, after the rejoicings and felicitations had died away, the dens quietly re-opened without the usual signboard and smoking went on as before. Spasms of prohibition have failed and only the process of pinching off the evil by a gradually tightening ligature of permits and licenses has succeeded.

19) *Eradication of the cultivation of the poppy*
(Sir A. Hosie, *On the Trail of the Opium Poppy*, II, pp. 287–8)

In a word, the result of my investigation in the three northern provinces of China was that in 1910 poppy cultivation had been completely eradicated in Shansi, and that there had been a reduction of 30 and 25 per cent respectively in Shensi and Kansu as compared with the year 1907. As regards the three south-western provinces, cultivation had ceased in Szechuan in 1911, while Yünnan and Kueichou had reduced their cultivation in the same year by 75 and 70 per cent respectively. This was, on the whole, a notable achievement which was, however, nullified by the outbreak of the revolution in October, 1911, when the Central and Provincial Governments lost control and were unable, for the time being, to prevent a recrudescence of poppy cultivation.

20) *Schools for girls*
(Margaret E. Burton, *The Education of Women in China*, pp. 125–7)
Modern education even found its way into the districts beyond the cities. As early as 1906 a Tientsin missionary who had been making a study of the Chinese schools for girls in and about Tientsin wrote:

'But the most astounding discovery in girls' schools was not made in ... [Tientsin] but on a missionary country trip one hundred li from the city. We had previously travelled through the mud village of Pei-yeng-chiao and had mentally dubbed it "The White Pig Village", since the pigs were not of the usual Chinese variety. A native pastor in a neighbouring village informed us that there was actually a modern girls' school in this forlorn hamlet. ... In the inner court the teacher herself met us and offered her hand in foreign style. As we entered the school room the pupils arose. They were evidently frightened at the appearance of two outlandish foreigners and much relieved when we were conducted into the teacher's own sanctum – a tastefully fitted up inner room.

Over the usual teacups we said, "We have visited the government schools in Tientsin and wish to see if this admirable school is similarly arranged." To this she replied, "This is a miserable hamlet and cannot be compared with a city school." "What is your honourable school's schedule of studies?" "Only a few ordinary lessons," and thereupon she placed before us an elaborate program for every day, much like that of a Western school. The "few ordinary lessons" included etiquette, Chinese language, arithmetic, geography, elementary science, sewing, drawing, calisthenics and music.'

21) *The Chinese commitment to reform*
(Henri Borel, *The New China*, pp. 126, 131–2)

In Peking one can see better than in any city of the south how much reform has been achieved in a few years, especially during the last four years. The streets used to be full of puddles in which one risked breaking his neck; in the evening they were scarcely lighted by the paper lanterns, and very often unsafe as well. Everywhere there was dirt and water and a population hostile to the foreigner and to all foreign novelties. Now they are busy macadamising the roads, steam rollers are everywhere at work, the entire city has electric light, telephone wires are hung. Nowhere does one hear insulting words to Europeans; and an efficient body of police keeps order. Pure water is conducted to the city from the western hills. Bicycles and motor-cars drive through the streets, smart postmen of the Chinese Imperial Post Office distribute the letters, and a splendid fire-brigade of three hundred men guards against conflagrations.

Especially do the excellent police-force and the fire-brigade, organised by the liberal Manchu Prince Su, excite the admiration of the European press. Peking has now three railway stations, one at each of its lines – one from Tientsin, one from Mukden, and one from Kalgan. That of the Mukden line, the terminus of the Manchuria-Siberia-Europe, was built entirely after European models. [...]

Education now works for the future, and its seed comes up a million-fold. Not before this seed sprouts will the people of China be ripe for a Parliament. I still hear the words of one of my friends, a mandarin of the third degree. 'You must not laugh at our people,' he said, 'when it still says and does stupid things. It is a child just awakened. We must teach it, before it can rule itself.'

These last words were spoken with a voice in which vibrated something very genuine, with an amount of emotion that a Chinese seldom shows to a European. My friend is a highly-civilised Chinese who has the M.A. (Cantab.) and M.I.C.E. after his name, and who has lived a European life for years in Paris and London. One must be absolutely unfeeling, or a European obstinately convinced of his own superiority, not to sympathise with the modern patriotic sentiment, so fiercely real and so unselfishly beautiful, of an educated young Chinese.

22) *The Provincial Assemblies*
(*The Correspondence of G.E. Morrison*, pp. 532–4)

Peking, 6 December 1909

... I formed as have most correspondents a high opinion of the Provincial Assemblies I saw those in Tai Yuan Fu and in Hsi An Fu. They were conducted with a quiet decorum that was most promising. It is an important step in advance and I had hoped would be encouraged by *The Times* as the first instance of the provinces being given an opportunity to express in public assembly their views as to the needs of the province. . . . Bland however I see in a paper which he has sent you and of which he has left me a copy undated takes a very pessimistic view of the Assemblies saying that the spirit which animates them is patriotic in the sense that it denounces everything foreign. . . .
[. . .]

... I take the view that one of the most striking features of Modern China is the growth in national wealth security and prosperity and in the friendliness of the people towards foreign ways and foreign things. Bland however sees the country on the verge of bankruptcy and says that America is coming to the carcase to be here when it is divided among the powers. I think the country well suited for Constitutional Government and I consider that the trial of the Provincial Assemblies has been a conspicuous success and that to condemn China because she has instituted these Assemblies saying that 90% of the Manchus at least and 75% of the Chinese *literati* have never had any intention of upsetting the 'established order of things' seems to me unjust to a degree.

Most of the Provincial Assemblies elected as Chairman one of the *literati* and it has been quite remarkable how easily the delegates have entered upon their duties and how orderly they have been in debate. At every Assembly tables are provided for the reporters and it has been quite curious how fully reported have been the proceedings.

23) *The interior of China still under the torpor of the ages*
(E.J. Dingle, *Across China on Foot*, pp. 187–8)

In the Far Eastern and European press so much is heard of the awakening of China that one is apt really to believe that the whole Empire, from its Dan to Beersheba, is boiling for reform. But it may be that the husk is taken for the kernel. The husk comprises the treaty ports and some of the capital cities of tl e provinces; the kernel is that vast sleepy interior of China. Few people, even in Shanghai, know what it means; so that to the stay-at-home European pardon for ignorance of existing conditions so much out of his focus should readily be granted.

From Shanghai, up past Hankow, on to Ichang, through the Gorges to Chung-king, is a trip likely to strike optimism in the breast of the most sceptical foreigner. But after he has lived for a couple of years in an interior city as I have done, with its antiquated legislation, its superstition and idolatry, its infanticide, its girl suicides, its public corruption and moral degradation, rubbing shoulders continually at close quarters with the inhabitants, and himself living in the main a Chinese life, our optimist may alter his opinions, and stand in wonder at the extraordinary differences in the most ordinary details of life at the ports on the China coast and the Interior, and of the gross inconsistencies in the Chinese mind and character. If in addition he has stayed a few days away from a city in which the foreigners were shut up inside the city walls because the roaring mob of rebels outside were asking for their heads . . . he may increase his wonder to doubt. The aspect here in Yün-nan – politically, morally, socially, spiritually – is that of another kingdom, another world. Conditions seem, for the most part, the same yester-day, to-day, and for ever. And in his new environment, which may be a replica of twenty centuries ago, the dream he dreamed is now dispelled. 'China,' he says, 'is *not* awaking; she barely moves, she is still under the torpor of the ages.'

24) *Use of the telegraph in Hupei*
(A. Little, *Gleanings from Fifty Years in China*, pp. 30–1)
Doubtless, there is a leaven at work in our presence in China, which will in time leaven the mass, and the more points of contact, in the shape of treaty ports are created, the quicker will be the advance, but to the outward eye only a small radius round each port has been so far affected. It is true that the electric wire now unites in its bonds all the chief cities of the eighteen provinces, but its use, except always at the treaty ports, is almost always entirely confined to the carriage of official despatches. . . . In the case of the telegraph, the charges are high, averaging about one shilling a word, more or less, according to distance. This tariff is . . . quite prohibitive as far as social messages

are concerned; and for business purposes its use is confined to the few wealthy merchants in the larger towns, and by them used very sparingly. . . .

At one such station, in the town of Shin-tan in Hupeh, we once tried to send a message. After much inquiry we at last found our way to the Tien-pao-chü, or 'lightning despatch office,' and were shown to an old out-of-the-way two-storied Chinese dwelling-house. . . . As our eyes gradually grew accustomed to the dim light admitted through the small paper windows, we perceived in one corner a curtained trestle bedstead illuminated by a diminutive opium-smoker's lamp, in another corner a telegraphic signalling instrument with a silk cover to protect it from the dirt. . . . As we entered, a man of thirty, handsomely dressed in silk, arose from the bed and welcomed us to a seat. He received us with great effusion and, to our surprise, seemed really pleased to see his haunt invaded by a barbarian. A lad of eighteen or less, also gaily dressed in silks, produced the hospitable tea, and conversation commenced. The manager could not accept my message without a card from the Taotai, or Governor, who resided forty miles distant and with which he advised me to provide myself on a future occasion. The lad, who turned out to be an operator trained in Shanghai, had merely to report on the condition of the wires, which he did daily by telegraphing to the next station the English words 'all right.' The rest of the English he once knew he appeared to have forgotten.

25) *The survival of the social system in Weihaiwei*
(R.F. Johnston, *Lion and Dragon in Northern China*, pp. 139–40)
Weihaiwei has as yet shown but little tendency to modify its semi-patriarchal social system as a consequence of its fifteen years of continuous contact with Western civilisation. The individual is still sunk in the family. He cannot divest himself of the rights any more than of the responsibilities that belong to him through his family membership. The Weihaiwei farmer has indeed so limited a conception of his own existence as a separate and distinct personality that in ordinary speech he continually confuses himself with his ancestors or with living members of his family. Examples of this are of repeated occurrence in the law-courts. 'I bought this land and now the Tung family is trying to steal it from me,' complains a petitioner. 'When did you buy it?' asks the magistrate. 'Two hundred years ago,' promptly

replies the oppressed one. Says another, 'My rights to the property of Sung Lien-têng are being contested by my distant cousin. I am the rightful owner. I buried Sung Lien-têng and have charge of his soul-tablet and carry out the ancestral ceremonies.' 'When did Sung Lien-têng die?' questions the magistrate. 'In the fortieth year of K'ang Hsi' is the reply. This means that the deceased whose property is in dispute died childless in 1701, that plaintiff's ancestor in that year defrayed the funeral expenses and acted as chief mourner, that by family agreement he was installed as adopted son to the deceased and heir to his property, and that plaintiff claims to be the adopted son's descendant and heir. Looking upon his family, dead and alive, as one and indivisible, he could not see any practical difference between the statement that certain funeral rites had been carried out by himself and the statement that they had been carried out by a direct ancestor.

THE 1911 REVOLUTION AND THE ERA OF THE WARLORDS

The overthrow of the Manchus and the establishment of a republic was treated by westerners with a combination of equanimity and levity. George Lanning, former Principal of the Shanghai Public School recorded the scene in Shanghai when the revolution broke out there (1). Frederick McCormick described the consequences of the passage of legislation in December 1911 making optional the wearing of the queue, the symbol of subservience to the Manchus (2). Daniele Varè, an Italian diplomat, poked fun at the formal dress now thought appropriate by Chinese officials (3).

Western estimates of the new leadership varied. J.O.P. Bland wrote dismissively of Sun Yat-sen, first President of the Republic (4). His opinion contrasted with that of Dr James Cantlie, formerly Dean of the College of Medicine in Hong Kong from where Sun had graduated (5).

For some westerners, the establishment of the Chinese Republic was part of a 'great awakening' sweeping over Asia. George Sherwood Eddy accompanied Dr John Mott on a seven-month evangelizing mission to Asia on behalf of the Missionary Education Movement in America. He was very enthusiastic about the changes taking place in China, emphasizing the strength of patriotic feeling and the role of Christianity (6). J.S. Thomson, echoing the optimism of a century earlier, hailed the commercial opportunities which the revolution offered to the United States (7). By contrast, G. Lowes Dickinson and Richard Wilhelm saw in China the preservation of the spiritual certainties which Europe, torn by war, had lost (8 and 9). Eric

Teichman, a British consular officer, who toured Shensi and Kansu in 1917, offered a very different view, for he described the effects of the 'White Wolf' rebellion, a harbinger of disorder in the warlord period between 1916 and 1928 (10).

O.D. Rasmussen noted the economic effect of the First World War on the foreign trade of Tientsin (11). The decision taken at Versailles, confirming Japanese possession of the former German interests in Shantung, triggered off the May Fourth demonstrations described by the educationalist John Dewey (12).

The period from the fall of the Empire until the outbreak of the Sino-Japanese War was the high point of western influence in China. J.O.P. Bland doubted that the Chinese were capable of organizing their own effective modern government and suggested a complete take-over of China's national finances by the western powers (13). Few westerners adopted so openly racist a tone towards the Chinese as did A.F. Legendre, a French doctor and late director of the Imperial School of Medicine at Chengtu (14). The decline into warlordism was graphically related by John Earl Baker who had been Adviser to the Chinese Ministry of Communications between 1916 and 1926 (15).

Views more sympathetic to ordinary Chinese were now being expressed. Mary Gamewell described the life of rickshaw coolies in Shanghai (16). Nora Waln went to China in 1920 and fell in love with the traditional life-style of an extended family living beside the Grand Canal (17). Somerset Maugham contrasted the privileges of Europeans with the harsh existence of Chinese coolies (18). Vera Vladimirovna Vishnyakova-Akimova was acutely embarrassed to find that employees of the Soviet embassy in Peking were still using rickshaws for transport (19).

The weakness of central government allowed westerners to penetrate remote areas. Harry Franck, who had already travelled the world, spent two years casually roving through China. He described himself as 'an average individual with no particular bent for the scientific or statistical, nor with an ax to grind'. He visited Taiyüan, and interviewed one of the best-known of the warlords, Yen Hsi-shan, the 'Model Governor' of the province of Shensi. In southern China his travels took him to the Sze Yap – the 'four districts' near Canton, from which most emigrants to the United States came (20 and 21).

In the mid-1920s, western observers in China were divided in their views on how China had changed since the revolution. Many concurred with the opinion expressed by Rodney Gilbert in *What's Wrong with China?* – which was that everything had gone wrong (22). But Paul Monroe described this as 'the point of view of the disillusioned', held by Old China Hands and the foreign business community – a case of what he called 'Shanghai-itis'. Monroe taught Chinese students at Columbia University, New York. He hoped that the student movement, for all its faults, would contribute effectively to the reconstruction of China under the leadership of the new Nationalist government (23). The direct riposte to Rodney Gilbert came from O.D. Rasmussen who dedicated his book *What's Right with China* to 'the young men and women of China whose exalted idealism is leading their country from the stagnant marshes of an alien-imposed regression to the hard highway of progress' (24).

In the 1920s western academics had the opportunity to carry out research and to write textbooks which placed China alongside other countries as an object of study. A pioneering example of this was the social survey of Peking carried out by Sidney Gamble and J.S. Burgess. Their quantified information covered many aspects of social life in Peking, including the prevalence of the 'social evil' (25). F.H. King conducted a systematic review of agricultural practices in China, and, in a generation before environmental issues gained prominence, stressed the importance of the Chinese model of permanent agriculture (26). The best-known study of rural China was that of John Lossing Buck, who submitted his findings of a survey of 2,866 farms for the degree of Doctor of Philosophy at Cornell University – seldom can a higher degree have been awarded for greater application! (27) Daniel Kulp, while praising this type of endeavour, asked 'Can it be said that apples are more important than girls, or wheat than boys?' – implying the need for a 'community analysis' of Chinese society, 'similar in adequacy and completeness to the agricultural studies'. His survey of a village in south China included a section on recreation (28). A fresh perspective on China's past came from archaeological investigations, particularly the discovery of the remains of the archaic hominid which became known as Peking Man (29). Meanwhile, the Buddhist art of Tunhuang was threatened with despoliation, and this prompted Langdon

Warner of the Fogg Art Museum at Harvard to use the methods of rescue archaeology to try to preserve part of it (30).

1) *The Revolution in Shanghai*
(George Lanning, *Old Forces in New China*, pp. 313–15)
... On the very day on which the first constitution was offered, 3rd November, Shanghai was taken possession of by the revolutionary party. Not even the taking of Hanyang had proved a simpler task. The insurgents came, saw, and conquered. Only at the Kiangnan Arsenal situated a mile or two westward from the native city was there any resistance. Here the guard thought it incumbent on them to make some show of resistance, and a few shots were fired, but very few minutes had elapsed before it was seen that the revolutionists had a simple task before them, and they were soon able to congratulate themselves on having secured possession of all that a great arsenal stands for.... It was during a Friday eve and night that these events took place, and few Shanghai residents are likely ever to forget the altered scene which presented itself on the following morning. Foreign merchants driving in from the West End to business found the Maloo, (the main thoroughfare) a mass of dazzling white. Every house had its flag, ranging in area from many square yards of white sheeting to the tiniest scrap of rag which was all that some poor people could find for the occasion. ...

There was no doubt as to the popularity of the political change. Never before had the foreigner seen such an assemblage of bright and smiling native faces as were exhibited in Shanghai on Saturday, 4th November 1911. At last, it was believed that China was once more to be governed by Chinese. At last the end of the terrible lane was in sight. All the many provincials who meet in that great commercial emporium, the foreign settlement at Shanghai, fraternized in most unwonted fashion, and the foreigner was felt to be the friend of all. There was little difficulty in arranging for the maintenance of law and order. Revolutionaries took charge of the native city, the representative Taotai of the Manchu *régime* taking sanctuary in the Settlement whose interests he had not always been over-willing to forward. The control of the Mixed Court in the so-called English Settlement was placed, for the time being and to its unspeakable advantage, in the hands of the Shanghai Municipality, and in general there arose a spirit of friendliness between native and foreign authorities which was highly satisfactory. . . .

2) *Queue-cutting parties*
(Frederick McCormick, *The Flowery Republic*, pp. 367–8)

To me the first signs of real queue-cutting came at Tientsin. It reached the college-prank state at Shanghai – which had been the centre of the anti-opium-pipe crusade – and became a popular diversion at Canton. It was of the nature of a City festival, lasting several days. I am sure that more queues fell in this campaign of shears than did opium pipes in the opium crusade. There was a flash in the sunlight, a snip, and gone was the glistening braid.

In a City of two and a quarter millions not a queue was visible in the streets after three days. Citizens who were determined to hold on to their ancient and honourable appendages remained in seclusion and fear. It was a gala day for all those Republicans who could arm themselves with shears. They paraded the streets ready to sunder every queue. Shopkeepers joined the groups and mobs of queue-cutting outlaws, all good-natured, awaiting the unsuspecting victims – carriers, chair-bearers, teachers, salesmen, farmers. Clip, and off came the victim's queue – his mortification greeted with howls of delight from the crowd. It was a kind of daylight 'Boston Tea Party,' in the Canton style. [. . .]

There was no becoming accustomed to this 'new' China. There was no time. Discarding queues only gave it a taste: it began changing its dress, and here the women joined in – foreign headgear, walking-sticks, umbrellas, and if you please, foreign clothes. The demand for foreign-cut clothes was so great that a large fan-shop slack of work at that season – late autumn – opened a cap factory and did a thriving business. The foreign-style tailors, who had been obliged heretofore to subsist on a meagre trade with the foreigner, were so beset by native customers that foreign residents of Canton could get nothing.

3) *Foreign fashion*
(Daniele Varè, *Laughing Diplomat*, pp. 94–5)

Thursday, 30th January [1913] . . .

A big ball last night at the French Legation. Since the Chinese have given up their old official robes and national costume, you never know how they will dress for these functions. Last night there were two young sparks in grey flannel trousers, tennis shoes, tunics of black satin, blue sun-spectacles and fur caps with the ear-flaps dangling down on each side. Most of the others wore ordinary evening dress with white tie. Some of their swallow-tailed coats and black trousers were lined with fur, which did not improve the cut. The old Chinese dress was always fur-lined in winter, as the houses were warmed only with an occasional brazier. The fur-lined dress-suits that the Chinese officials put on now, when they come out to foreign evening parties, must be far too warm for steam-heated rooms and leave the wearer's chest unprotected except by a starched shirt-front. Yet the wearers don't put on coats when they go out. I wonder they don't all get pneumonia. The shirt represents the greatest difficulty for the Chinaman who dresses 'foreign fashion' for the first time. We had proof of this at the French Legation ball. There was a tubby Chinese official whose shirt-front bulged out of his waistcoat; it appeared to be several sizes too large for him. I might not have noticed this myself, but I saw my Chief staring at the little Chinese, with an expression of indignant astonishment. Then he turned to me and said:

'When I get home, I'm going to sack the washerman!'

'What has he done now?' I asked.

'That man is wearing a shirt of mine,' was the answer. 'There is my crest embroidered under the starched front. Now I understand why our evening shirts remain at the wash for weeks on end. The washerman hires them out!'

4) *Sun Yat-sen*

(J.O.P. Bland, *Recent Events and Present Policies in China*, pp. 224–5)

In many ways he recalls the character of Danton. He is more of a visionary and idealist than the great Jacobin, and less of a politician; but he resembles him in the restless and energetic temperament of the born conspirator. Like him, he is no believer in promiscuous bloodshed, and recognises the necessity for soothing and allaying the lawless spirit of insurrection evoked by the Revolution, and for reconciling civil hatreds in the State. He has all Danton's incapacity for practical administration, combined with his optimistic belief in the reformation of humanity by force of institutions, and a robust faith in himself as the Heaven-sent Reformer. But here the resemblance ends.

The methods by which Sun Yat-sen would set China's house in order are peculiarly his own; they reflect an almost European ignorance of Chinese history and the dreamer's disregard for everything which fails to square with his own hypotheses and ideals.

There can be no doubt as to his considerable influence with the Radical extremists of the Cantonese party, and especially with the politically-active Chinese communities overseas. His personal relations with the latter class, from which have been drawn most of the funds of the T'ung Meng-hui, is in itself sufficient to account for his ascendancy with the small clique of youthful politicians which successfully forced through the abolition of the Monarchy. In addition to the prestige which he enjoys in the eyes of Young China as a much-travelled and well-educated man, the personal magnetism to which many observers have testified, and a wide-spread reputation for sincerity and honesty, have sufficed to raise him well above the ordinary level of the place-seeking politicians.

There is a certain large vagueness, a splendid indefiniteness about Dr. Sun Yat-sen's reform schemes that, were it not for the *naïve* sincerity of the man himself, would make them and him ridiculous. But he believes in himself, with the whole-souled and rapt belief of a child building sand-castles, and the valour of his ignorance is passing brave. He believes in universal suffrage and votes for Chinese women. He believes in Lloyd George and Henry George; in the single tax and conscription; in the nationalisation of railways; and he promises the Chinese people (which hear him not) every kind of rare and refreshing fruit, to be produced without the formality of planting trees.

5) *In defence of Sun Yat-sen*
(J. Cantlie and C.S. Jones, *Sun Yat Sen*, pp. 140–2)
The chief reason of Sun Yat Sen being held up to something approaching ridicule by the Legations, the officials of the Imperial Maritime Customs, the Consuls, the Old China hands, and the 'authorities' on 'things Chinese,' who advised the Press in Europe, was that a republic in China was an impossibility, and that any man who could think of such a thing must be a dreamer, a faddist, and a danger to China. When the revolution broke out in November, 1911, the idea that it was serious was ridiculed by those whom the Press consulted in the matter.

These 'authorities' stated that a revolution of the kind in China occurred every fifty years, that one was now due, that the present outbreak was merely a 'recurring row,' and that the men concerned in it, and Sun Yat Sen in particular, were of no importance in the eyes of the Chinese Government, the foreign Legations, the Customs officials, and the bankers, &c., in China. The true reason of this belief was that the representatives of the Press consulted men whose experience of China was confined to Government ways and doings or to the assertions of foreigners in China in touch with officials. Another almost universally stated and credited opinion was that the Chinese, saturated with worship of a throne and respect for its edicts, could never become a republic. Moreover, that they were not ready for a republic, being wholly uneducated in the ways of government.

6) *The New Era in China*
(G.S. Eddy, *The New Era in Asia*, pp. 121–2)
On our arrival at Shanghai a banquet was given to welcome Dr Mott and myself. It was a sight to see the leaders of this young Republic, arrayed in evening dress, gathering in the Palace Hotel some two hundred strong. In the chair was Mr K.S. Wong, business-manager of China's great Iron and Steel Works, and perhaps the future Carnegie of China. In his works, employing over 5000 workmen, we saw skilled labourers turning out the finest of steel rails wherewith to build the new railways of China, which will stretch from Shanghai to Burma and from Canton in the south to Siberia in the north. On the left sat the celebrated Dr Wu Ting-fang, formerly Minister in Washington, who represented the revolutionary forces in the negotiations with the Manchus at the formation of the new Republic of China. Next to him sat the manager of the Nanking Railway, a graduate of Yale. Though not a Christian, he said: 'Confucianism has supplied China with precepts in the past, but China imperatively needs Christianity to-day to furnish her with moral power. Many leading men are now turning toward Christianity as the hope of China; it is a sign of the times.' Others gave the same testimony.

On Dr Mott's right at the banquet sat a Confucianist who had made a six hours' journey to Shanghai, as the special representative of the governor of Hangchow, to ask for a Young Men's Christian Association building and officially to request the organization of an Association in their city, the governor promising to give the site.

7) Get ready for the China trade
(J.S. Thomson, *China Revolutionized*, pp. 137–9)
The eastern states of America and Great Britain have a new slogan: 'Get ready for the Panama Canal.' The western states of America, and indeed all America, should have another slogan: 'Get ready for the China trade.'. . .

On my travels and life of three years in China, I have listened, and I have glanced about for signs of the new times; and I shall relate just a few of the indications of progress. . . .

Agricultural machinery will before long be required on the great plains of Pechili, Mongolia and the three Manchurian provinces, whence America will draw much grain, meat, oil, lumber and coal. Nail, needle and glass factories are going up on a small scale. China has the iron in the mine, but she will need our machinery. Paper mills are largely increasing, and we need their pulp. . . . Factories making soap, the most glaringly deficient thing in dirty China hitherto, have been erected, even in far western Chingtu City. . . . Woolen mills have been erected at Shanghai, Peking, Lanchow, Hankau, Kalgan, etc., to work up the vast supplies of Mongolian and Pechili shearings. . . . Hardware and enameled ware factories have been erected at Tientsin, Canton, etc., but China can not for years take care of her needs in hardware. . . . All of these industries need machinery. Of all municipal improvements, China has needed modern water-works the most. . . . In little of this have the Americans entered as yet, though they will on a vast scale as American finance and industry extends its agencies.

8) On T'ai-shan, China's sacred mountain
(G. Lowes Dickinson, *Appearances*, pp. 99–101)
When lovers of China – 'pro-Chinese,' as they are contemptuously called in the East – assert that China is more civilised than the modern West, even the candid Westerner, who is imperfectly acquainted with the facts, is apt to suspect insincere paradox. Perhaps these few notes on Tai Shan may help to make the matter clearer. A people that can consecrate a place of natural beauty is a people of fine feeling for the essential values of life. That they should also be dirty, disorganised,

corrupt, incompetent, even if it were true – and it is far from being true in any unqualified sense – would be irrelevant to this issue. On a foundation of inadequate material prosperity they reared, centuries ago, the superstructure of a great culture. The West, in rebuilding its foundations, has gone far to destroy the superstructure. Western civilisation, wherever it penetrates, brings with it water-taps, sewers, and police; but it brings also an ugliness, an insincerity, a vulgarity never before known to history, unless it be under the Roman Empire. It is terrible to see in China the first wave of this Western flood flinging along the coasts and rivers and railway lines its scrofulous foam of advertisements, of corrugated iron roofs, of vulgar, meaningless architectural forms. In China, as in all old civilisations I have seen, all the building of man harmonises with and adorns nature. In the West everything now built is a blot. . . . The ugliness of the West is a symptom of a disease of the Soul. It implies that the end has been lost sight of in the means. In China the opposite is the case. The end is clear, though the means be inadequate. Consider what the Chinese have done to Tai Shan, and what the West will shortly do, once the stream of Western tourists begins to flow strongly. Where the Chinese have constructed a winding stairway of stone, beautiful from all points of view, Europeans or Americans will run up a funicular railway, a staring scar that will never heal. Where the Chinese have written poems in exquisite caligraphy, *they* will cover the rocks with advertisements. Where the Chinese have built a series of temples, each so designed and placed as to be a new beauty in the landscape, *they* will run up restaurants and hotels like so many scabs on the face of nature. I say with confidence that they *will*, because they *have* done it wherever there is any chance of a paying investment. Well, the Chinese need, I agree, our science, our organisation, our medicine. But is it affectation to think they may have to pay too high a price for it, and to suggest that in acquiring our material advantages they may lose what we have gone near to lose, that fine and sensitive culture which is one of the forms of spiritual life? The West talks of civilising China. Would that China could civilise the West!

9) *The music of Suchou*
(Richard Wilhelm, *The Soul of China* pp. 255–7)
. . . The spring seemed to ring through the remnant of the day. There was a sound: a thin sweet sound in the midst of the chaos of the street. A

few pricked up their ears for a moment, whilst others hurried on. The sounds of spring approached. It penetrated the noise of the street quite clearly like a shimmering golden thread; a melody was heard with that sweet sad strain which makes you suspect autumn in spring. It was almost painfully beautiful. A blind man was playing soft notes upon a Chinese violin. Wherever he passed men ceased to speak of money, the children stopped their games and the tired wanderer stood still for a moment. The song of spring flowed like magic from the violin of the blind man. His vision was turned inwards.

He accepted no gifts. He played and passed on. His melody vanished slowly in the distance. In the meantime night had fallen and the world with its bustling people and dusky houses was there once more, and only high above persisted the sound of the little bells of the pagoda.

In the town there is a garden: one of those magical Chinese gardens where you wander in a labyrinth amidst ponds, rocks, pavilions and groves, where every step presents a new picture to the eye. Formerly the garden was hedged in by solitude. It lay beyond the gates of the town. To-day the railway station and ugly inns for passing visitors are situated in its vicinity. After we had derived an idea of the beauty of China, all the ugliness of Europe grinned at us once more. People sometimes speak of the animosity of the Chinese to aliens. The Chinese are not at all hostile to foreigners. They merely defend themselves against the mire which emanating from the West threatens to choke the world. . . .

But China will not die. It possesses the power to save itself from the 'White Peril', and there are men who have the faculty of understanding the nature of European culture, of distinguishing it from those expressions of what is ugly in it. In Shanghai an invitation to a Chinese restaurant awaited me. . . . A small group of artists and scholars met to partake of a choice meal. . . . The painter Ch'en Chu Ts'ung, the leader of the modern Chinese painters . . . gave in a few sentences a survey of the modern artistic movement. . . . He has assimilated in a perfectly free manner, on the basis of the Chinese technique of ink drawing, the stimulus supplied by French artists, and he has created from it a new national Chinese art. . . .

10) *The 'White Wolf' rebellion*
(Eric Teichman, *Travels of a Consular Officer in North-West China*,
pp. 22–4)
The number of burnt-out ruins of hamlets, farmsteads, and huts along
the trail we had just traversed could not fail to attract one's notice, and
enquiries elicited the fact that these were the result of the passage of
the terrible 'White Wolf' rebels, who passed in and out of Shensi in
scattered bands by these out of the way mountain trails in 1914.
During our wanderings through Shensi and Kansu we often found
ourselves travelling in the footsteps of this devastating horde, whose
trail of desolation could be traced . . . from the borders of Honan to
the confines of the Kokonor. Their lootings, burnings, and killings
recall the depredations of the T'aip'ing and Mahomedan rebels who
devastated N.W. China, south and north of the Ch'inling Shan
respectively, fifty years ago.

This terrible horde of bandits or rebels was an aftermath of the
rebellion of 1913. It consisted of an organized and well-equipped
nucleus of a few thousand fighting men, disbanded soldiery from the
Yangtzu Valley and Secret Society men from Honan, together with
many thousands of local adherents drawn from amongst the brigands,
soldiers and bad characters of the provinces through which they
passed. The four words 'Pai Lang Chao Liang' (White Wolf is
recruiting) passed secretly up and down the Han Valley, and recruits
from all quarters flocked to join the band. After 30,000 of Yuan
Shih-k'ai's best Northern troops had failed to crush these rebels in
Honan, they burst through into the Han valley *via* the rich mart of
Laoho K'ou, where a foreign missionary was murdered in the sacking
of the city, and early in 1914 worked through the mountains into
Central Shensi. Hsian, with its mighty walls, withstood the raiders as it
had withstood the Mahomedans fifty years earlier, and the horde drove
on almost unopposed through Western Shensi into Southern Kansu,
looting, burning and killing. The massacres of Chinese non-
combatants were appalling, and the raiders, many of them mere
youths, richly dressed in looted silks and jewellery and armed with
modern rifles and Mauser pistols, rivalled in their cruelty and lust for
indiscriminate slaughter the most terrible of Chinese rebels of days
gone by. The object of the raid into the North West seems to have
been the stocks of opium in Shensi and Kansu. The resistance they

met with and the measures taken to deal with them reflect no credit on the Chinese Government. . . . It was not until they reached the Mahomedan districts of Kansu near the Kokonor border that they suffered any serious loss. . . . Eventually the survivors straggled back with their loot through Shensi to their homes in Honan and Anhui. The Chinese officials assert that White Wolf himself, who appears to have been an ex-military officer from the Yangtzu armies, was captured and executed.

11) *Trade in the war years at Tientsin*
(O.D. Rasmussen, *Tientsin*, pp. 289–91)
Despite the war in Europe the trade of 1914 showed an increase over 1913, while the Revenue, not quite 5 per cent, was double the figures of ten years before, 1904. Fear of German cruisers at large in the China seas caused a temporary suspension of shipping in August and September, while increased marine insurance rates told heavily against importers. Matters seemed as though they would come to a standstill until activity in the export market set in during the autumn. A blockade of Tsingtao increased exports by way of Tientsin. The boom was so great that not enough ships were found to carry the cargo away. The net value of trade in 1914 fell 10,000,000 taels under 1913, due largely to the falling off of munitions imports, owing to foreign embargoes and danger of capture as contraband. The decline of Taels 3,000,000 in exports was attributed to the high rate of exchange and depredations of the 'Pai Lang', or White wolf in Honan, Shansi and Kansu, also to unrest in Mongolia. There was a phenomenal export of beans and peas; a brisk demand for walnuts and a war demand for goatskins in large quantities to be made into coats and sleeping bags for soldiers in France. Tanned goat skins fell off owing to the tanneries of the United States not being able to obtain proper quality of tanning dyes from blockaded Germany. Bristles also receded. The newly purchased Ice-breakers began their work on the river and opened it to traffic in 1914 on January 22nd. Another Ice-breaker was obtained in December. War exigencies, commandeering of British ships for war uses and consequent late delivery of cargoes destined for Tientsin prevented any big trading in 1915, but the figures were higher than in 1914. Exports increased owing to a brisk demand from abroad. Pack ice in the gulf interfered with shipping at Taku. The difficulty of

obtaining piece goods from abroad stimulated the Chinese to one of the most significant steps in their industrial life and one that will in the course of another decade turn China into an exporter of piece goods. They began to erect factories, equipped with foreign machinery and supervised by foreign experts. The output of these mills is much in favor among Chinese and increasingly so with foreigners. The inferior 'Made for Export' articles of Europe can no longer compete in style and durability with the native product, and if the Chinese are wise enough to refrain from adulterating their manufactures with 'shoddy', and stand by their low wage scale advantages, European piece goods, stockings, underwear and knitted goods will soon cease to find a market in China.

12) *Witnessing the birth of a nation*
(J. and A.C. Dewey, *Letters from China and Japan*, pp. 209–12)

PEKING, June 1.
We have just seen a few hundred girls march away from the American Board Mission school to go to see the President to ask him to release the boy students who are in prison for making speeches on the street. To say that life in China is exciting is to put it fairly. We are witnessing the birth of a nation, and birth always comes hard. . . . Yesterday we went to see the temples of Western Hills, conducted by one of the members of the Ministry of Education. As we were running along the big street that passes the city wall we saw students speaking to groups of people. This was the first time the students had appeared for several days. We asked the official if they would not be arrested, and he said, 'No, not if they keep within the law and do not make any trouble among the people.' This morning when we got the paper it was full of nothing else. The worst thing is that the University has been turned into a prison with military tents all around it and a notice on the outside that this is a prison for students who disturb the peace by making speeches. As this is all illegal, it amounts to a military seizure of the University and therefore all the faculty will have to resign. . . . The other thing we heard was that in addition to the two hundred students locked up in the Law Building, two students were taken to the Police rooms and flogged on the back. Those two students were making a speech and were arrested and taken before the officers of the gendarmerie. Instead of shutting up as they were expected to do, the boys asked some questions of these officers that were embarrassing to

answer. The officers then had them flogged on the back. . . . We saw students making speeches this morning about eleven, when we started to look for houses, and heard later that they had been arrested, that they carried tooth brushes and towels in their pockets. Some stories say that not two hundred but a thousand have been arrested. There are about ten thousand striking in Peking alone. The marching out of those girls was evidently a shock to their teachers and many mothers were there to see them off. The girls were going to walk to the palace of the President, which is some long distance from the school. If he does not see them, they will remain standing outside all night and they will stay there till he does see them. I fancy people will take them food. We heard the imprisoned students got bedding at four this morning but no food till after that time. There is water in the building and there is room for them to lie on the floor. They are cleaner than they would be in jail, and of course much happier for being together.

13) *China's officialdom more venal than ever before*
(J.O.P. Bland, *China Japan and Korea*, pp. 74–5)
Let us face the simple truth, which Young China's record of the past eight years has repeatedly emphasised, namely, that one thing, and one thing only, prevents the establishment of a stable Central Government at Peking, and this is the insatiable greed of money which possesses every Chinese who attains to public office. Take, for example, the record of the so-called Republican leaders who came to the front in 1911. Those who rose to high office as Tuchuns, speedily proved that a mandarin by any other name is still a mandarin. Almost without exception they proceeded to amass great fortunes at all costs and all speed. In the words of the *North China Daily News* (always a well-disposed observer), 'Chinese officialdom under the so-called democracy has become more irresponsible and more flagrantly venal than ever before'. . . .
Young China to-day, as in 1911, loudly proclaims its patriotic integrity of purpose and capacity for honest work in the public service; but the fact remains (and the Chinese themselves admit it) that it is not possible to name a dozen men in all the ranks of the bureaucracy, old or new, whose record would command implicit confidence in the matter of disinterested, clean-handed administration. It is because of the lack of such men, and the impossibility of reorganising a stable Government without them, that the great majority of patriotic, non-

official Chinese have come to the conclusion that the country's best chance of regaining stability and security lies in placing the national finances, as a whole, under some form of foreign supervision.

14) *The present condition of the Chinese mind*
(A.F. Legendre, *Modern Chinese Civilization*, pp. 167–70)
If now we examine the present condition of the Chinese mind, what do we see? The first and normal manifestation of a sound organ is its reactions to movement and activity: this is the necessary condition of regular functioning. It is desirable in the first place to consider how far the Chinaman possesses the most important of all forms of activity – the creative faculty.

The answer can be given in a few words: he has created nothing for 2,000 years, and, more than that, he seems incapable of bringing any industry whatever to perfection. Of late years, when employed by Europeans to work their machines, it was found that he learned quickly how to manage them and how to profit by them, but he could never suggest any improvement to them; on the contrary, if he were not continually stirred up and watched by the European, he would soon diminish their working efficiency by neglect.

Do we find in the physical state of the Chinaman any evidences of lack of cerebral activity? Yes; the Chinaman will pass from waking to sleeping with extraordinary ease; as soon as he ceases active occupation, his organs enter into physiological repose – he falls asleep. You may note this anywhere in China; if, for instance, he has been walking along the road and steps into a sedan chair, slumber instantly overtakes him.

His senses have not the same acuteness as those of the European; his sight and his hearing have not the same fineness or rapidity of perception; his sense of smell is very imperfect; certain evil-smelling substances make hardly any impression on his olfactory organs. . . .

One can affirm as a general rule without fear of error that the functioning powers of the different organs in the yellow man are inferior to those of the white. This commonplace is confirmed by physiological and pathological observation. I will cite only the fact that the blood circulates more slowly, and renders the organism less apt to defensive reactions.

15) *China's railway system under the warlords*
(John Earl Baker, *Explaining China*, pp. 220–4)

The new regime in 1912 set about improving the administration of the Government lines. These had been operated in 'water-tight compartments'; that is, each line had been operated as an independent entity. Trains arrived at and departed from junctions without reference to the trains of other lines. Passengers were required to buy their tickets separately for each line. . . . There was more coöperation between the railways of the different countries of Europe, up to the War, than between the different lines composing the Chinese Government railway system. . . .

The Republic called to the railway administration a considerable number of young men who had specialized abroad in that subject. Commissions composed of these, together with the technical heads of the various departments of the railways, were formed to remedy the conditions described above. A standard system of accounts was drawn up, together with provisions for appropriate statistics. Annual reports were published. A Traffic Conference arranged for through trains between important cities, through tickets and through checking of baggage. . . . Within eight years 'through invoicing' of goods and interchange of rolling stock had been arranged. The Ministry of Communications began to assume the functions pertaining to the head office of a railway system rather than those of a special bureau to relieve the Foreign Office of work in connection with foreign railway contractors.

The improved administration was accompanied by improved financial returns. . . . Revenues increased from $52,000,000 in 1915 . . . to $119,000,000 in 1923. . . .

But clouds of trouble had already appeared above the horizon. Political factions already were dissipating these large surpluses in the attempt to maintain their positions. Discipline on the lines was becoming difficult; pay-rolls were distended with useless appointees; the military were travelling free, lending their uniforms to friends, selling passes and carrying large quantities of commercial goods as military stores.

. . . At about the same time that Japan at the Washington Conference was agreeing to sell the Shantung railway to the Chinese Government, a military faction in control of the province of Honan was beginning to collect the railway revenues at the stations. This irregularity was corrected by the promise of the Ministry of Communications to pay over, monthly, a certain lump sum of money. Shortly afterwards the northern section of the Peking-Mukden railway was seized by the Manchurian forces. Soon the Tientsin-Pukow was forced to pay over, to the provincial armies in its neighbourhood, monthly sums equal to its net revenues.

These hardships made it impossible for the lines in question to pay interest and to meet their commitments for materials and additional equipment. The commercial service of the railways was not affected seriously, however, until the fall of 1924, when military forces practically seized the entire railway system. . . .

As these lines are being written [April, 1926] the Peking Mukden railway is under the control of two hostile factions. The Peking-Hankow Railway is also under the control of two different armies. The Tientsin Pukow line is under the control of three different factions. . . . The line from Wuchang to Changsha has fallen into such a state of disrepair that a speed of only eight miles per hour is permitted. Employees on the Peking-Suiyuan line are several months behind in their pay. . . .

The only line which uninterruptedly continues to serve the Chinese public is the South Manchuria Railway, which is protected by Japanese troops.

16) *Rickshaw coolies in Shanghai*
(Mary Ninde Gamewell, *The Gateway to China*, pp. 93–4, 98–9)
Wheelbarrow coolies, though, are said to live longer and fare better than most ricsha coolies. This latter class is very shortlived as a rule. Their working years do not ordinarily extend beyond three, five, or at the most ten. One Shanghai ricsha coolie declared he had pulled a ricsha for twenty-four years, but this, if true, was most exceptional. At the present time there are between nine and ten thousand public ricshas in Shanghai, but probably a shifting population during the year of many times that number of coolies. Some one who has studied the subject estimates that the entire coolie population of Shanghai, including all classes, reaches as high as four hundred thousand. The average earnings of a ricsha coolie are seven coppers, about three or four cents, a day, and from this pittance he must support a family, and that too in a city noted over China for high cost of living. No wonder a doctor in charge of a mission hospital where many sick coolies are sent

recently reported, 'A large number of the cases brought in are in a state of collapse due to malnutrition and the bad hygienic conditions of their life superadded to the strenuous spasmodic strain they undergo.' Heart trouble and China's inveterate foe, tuberculosis, carry off the majority. Perspiring freely, even in winter, after a hard run, then waiting, it may be an hour, for another 'fare,' in the penetrating wind or chilling rain, with no extra covering for their thinly clad bodies, the coolies are in a condition to succumb readily to disease. Married men live in colonies in the outskirts of the city, in little straw or bamboo huts, for which they pay a rental of from fifteen to twenty cents a month. In cold weather the whole family crawls inside to keep warm, where the air is heavy with tobacco smoke and the fumes from the little charcoal fire over which the rice is cooking. Many a baby contracts eye disease that later leads to blindness. Unmarried ricsha coolies sleep wherever they can find shelter, ordinarily in the cheap tea-houses, often as many as fifty herding together in one small room. The conditions in these places beggar description. [. . .]

It is interesting to see how quickly a fresh arrival from the West accustoms himself to ricsha riding. At first he is apt to inveigh against man-drawn vehicles, or if he gets into a ricsha, to sit lightly on the seat, with perhaps one foot hanging out at the side, with the idea of helping the coolie along, but presently he abandons himself to the enjoyment of the little, easy-running carriage, or as one enthusiastic woman described it 'a grown-up's perambulator,' and almost ceases to think of the puller as a human being. But let him stand on the Bund some day in the late afternoon and watch the stream of ricshas hurrying by. There is scarcely a coolie whose face is not drawn as if with pain, and many are actually contorted. Although a ricsha coolie's life is far from a bed of roses, in his own happy-go-lucky way he does manage to get some pleasure out of it. One of the ricsha companies, with benevolent intentions, undertook to furnish free hot tea to its men at the company's headquarters, but the plan didn't work, for the reason that the coolies preferred to buy their own tea at a tea-house. Wretched as is the low-class tea-house, it is the coolies' favorite gathering place, where, surrounded by their cronies, they can gossip, smoke, and gamble till necessity drives them forth to work again.

17) *Six generations under one roof*
(Nora Waln, *The House of Exile*, pp. 31–2)
From the moment of my arrival in China it was as though, like Alice, I
had stepped through a looking-glass into another world. The world I
left behind became a dim, fantastic dream. Only this into which I
entered seemed real. [. . .]

There are six generations of Lin now living. They dwell in
one-storey-high, single-room houses, which are built four-square
about a paved courtyard. The roofs extend well over the pillared
verandahs, which finish the front of each house, so that one can get
into a sedan chair in rainy weather without exposure to wet; and, after
their utilitarian duty is done, tilt upward in easy curves displaying fairy
scenes and fabulous creatures painted gaily under the eaves.

The houses have doors and windows only on one side, the side
opening into the court to which they belong. The homestead is
composed of sufficient courts to house comfortably the family, who are
eighty-three men, women and children at the time of this writing, and
to entertain in accord with their situation in society.

The courtyards are connected by gateways cut in the courtyard walls in
the shape of a flower, a fan, a vase, or a full moon. The courts, with their
dwelling rooms for the living, cluster around the double-roofed, storey-
and-a-half Hall of Ancestors, which shelters the life tablets of twenty-nine
generations of Lins, and their wives, who have 'plucked the flower of life.'

A protective grey wall, six feet thick and four times a man's height,
surrounds the homestead. The homestead neither overlooks nor is
overlooked by its neighbours. . . .

The 'Gate of Compassion,' a small window cut in the north wall,
where charity is given to the needy and the 'To and From the World
Gate,' a door of solid planks large enough for a horse and carriage to
be driven into the entrance court, are the only openings in the wall
connecting with the outside world.

18) *The beast of burden*
(W. Somerset Maugham, *On a Chinese Screen*, pp. 77–9)
At first when you see the coolie on the road, bearing his load, it is as a
pleasing object that he strikes the eye. In his blue rags, a blue of all
colours from indigo to turquoise and then to the paleness of a milky
sky, he fits the landscape. . . .

You see a string of coolies come along, one after the other, each with a pole on his shoulders from the ends of which hang two great bales, and they make an agreeable pattern. . . . You watch their faces as they pass you. They are good-natured faces and frank, you would have said, if it had not been drilled into you that the oriental is inscrutable; and when you see them lying down with their loads under a banyan tree . . . it seems natural to feel admiration for their endurance and their spirit. But you will be thought somewhat absurd if you mention your admiration to the old residents of China. You will be told with a tolerant shrug of the shoulders that the coolies are animals. . . .

The day wears on and it grows warmer. The coolies take off their coats and walk stripped to the waist. Then sometimes in a man resting for an instant, his load on the ground but the pole still on his shoulders so that he has to rest slightly crouched, you see the poor tired heart beating against the ribs: you see it as plainly as in some cases of heart disease in the out-patients' room of a hospital. It is strangely distressing to watch. Then also you see the coolies' backs. The pressure of the pole for long years, day after day, has made hard red scars, and sometimes even there are open sores, great sores without bandages or dressing that rub against the wood; but the strangest thing of all is that sometimes, as though nature sought to adapt man for these cruel uses to which he is put, an odd malformation seems to have arisen so that there is a sort of a hump, like a camel's, against which the pole rests. But beating heart or angry sore, bitter rain or burning sun notwithstanding, they go on eternally, from dawn to dusk, year in year out, from childhood to the extreme of age. You see old men without an ounce of fat on their bodies, their skin loose on their bones, wizened, their little faces wrinkled and apelike, with hair thin and grey; and they totter under their burdens to the edge of the grave in which at last they shall have rest. And still the coolies go, not exactly running, but not walking either, sidling quickly, with their eyes on the ground to choose the spot to place their feet, and on their faces a strained, anxious expression. You can make no longer a pattern of them as they wend their way. Their effort oppresses you. You are filled with a useless compassion.

19) *Using rickshaws like colonialists*
(Vera Vladimirovna Vishnyakova-Akimova, *Two Years in Revolutionary China 1925-1927*, pp. 28–9)
In front, in the shade of large trees, perhaps fifteen cheerful, white-toothed rickshaw men were sitting without embarrassment right on the sidewalk. Some of them had begun their breakfasts. They rapidly manipulated their chopsticks, holding their bowls at lip-level and joked with one another. All of them rushed towards us and we almost ran back to the embassy in fright to the great surprise of the gatekeeper.

We were astounded. Why were there rickshaws here? Was it possible that the embassy employees used rickshaws like the colonialists? Soon the situation was explained to us. It seemed that in the conditions of the time it was not always possible to act as one wished. An excessive straight-forwardness would have caused more harm than good. It was necessary to take the existent order into consideration. The first embassy employees did not want to use rickshaws. The very sight of such exploitation was repugnant to them. But the rickshaw men greeted this decision with hostility. They were being deprived of their wages. The embassy territory had been allotted to them and they demanded work. It almost caused a scandal. Employees coming out of the embassy were grabbed by rickshaw men who shoutingly demanded that they be hired. A delegation appeared at the embassy. The imperialists observed our difficult situation with delight. Thus instructions were given to hire rickshaws.

Soviet citizens behaved toward the rickshaw men in an entirely different manner from the representatives of the imperialist countries. We never disputed the fare and in general were much more generous. But most of all we viewed the rickshaw pullers as men, we never insulted their patriotic feelings or their personal dignity as did some 'civilized' representatives of the West who when paying would throw their money on the ground, as if recoiling from handing it over. Almost all of us had a personal rickshaw puller whom we didn't change. By the way, the friendship between one of our comrades and his rickshaw man unfortunately had a tragic ending. Seeing a hammer and sickle tattoo, the rickshaw man himself got tattooed this way. The rickshaw man paid cruelly for his indelible sympathy towards the Soviet Union after the 1927 raid on the embassy.

[From 1949 on employees of Soviet establishments again stopped using rickshaws.]

20) *The Model Governor*
(Harry A. Franck, *Wandering in Northern China*, pp. 260–4)
The governor received me one Sunday morning, with his civil secretary, the British-educated dean of the engineering department of the university, as interpreter. It seemed almost strange to walk so peacefully into his yamen through the same now rather tumble-down entrance at which more than twoscore foreigners were massacred by Boxer-influenced mobs in 1900. The governor prides himself on being a plain man and does not believe in surrounding himself with magnificence or formality.... Yet the essential Chinese courtesies were still there; there was no suggestion of a general surrender to Western bruskness. A solid-looking man, in physical as well as the other sense, with a somewhat genial face sunburned with evidence of his personal attention to his outdoor activities.... His garments were of cotton, not silk, and the simplicity of life this symbolizes has its effect upon his subordinates, at least in his presence.... He talked freely, yet certainly not boastfully, of his various policies, plain, common-sense policies, like the man himself, but which do not suggest themselves to the Chinese as readily as one might expect. Later I had opportunity to compare actual results with verbal intentions.

His laws against opium and bound feet would be better enforced, Yen Hsi-shan's friendly critics agree, if the officials under him were really in favor of such reforms. One man alone cannot cure a whole province, larger than most of our States, of the bad habits of generations. At first the governor was very assiduous on these points. Traffickers in, as well as growers of, the drug were fined and imprisoned, and life made as miserable as possible for those who persisted in consuming it. Inspectors examined the feet of women and assessed a fine of five dollars a year against those who had not unbound them, or who bound those of their daughters.... But the governor's [severity] is dying out, the people say, and little girls with bound feet may be seen near and even in Taiyüan....

The 'model governor' comes fairly near being a practical man in the Occidental sense. The forty automobiles in the government garages include huge streetcar-like buses that make good use of his new roads, and trucks that are run mainly by steam. Gasolene is expensive in Shansi and coal is cheap. Much of the city is taken up by what resembles immense barracks. . . . But if this gives the appearance of a ruler who considers the capital his private property, it makes possible a great normal school for all the province, where handcrafts are given proper attention, up-to-date soldiers' workshops, in which everything needed by the army is made, a model prison, and other spacious institutions on quite modern lines. [. . .]

All up and down the province the happy results of good rule are apparent. Village girls, like the boys who come to the various barrack-institutions in the capital, are taught what they are really likely to need in the life that in all probability lies before them, not the often useless stuff of an ideal but imaginary life, to which even American mission schools are somewhat prone. There are still such adversities as famine. . . . But even a civil and military governor combined cannot make rain fall.

21) *Sze Yap, the home of our own Chinese*
(Harry A. Franck, *Roving Through Southern China*, pp. 305–6, 308)
I came at length to a town called Kungyik, built a decade ago by returned emigrants. . . . Kungyik was a queer mixture of Chinese and foreign town, though on the whole there was no great evidence of Western influence. The streets were straight and properly narrow, but little less dirty than those of Canton, the town all in all disappointing to one who had heard so much of the improvements brought back from foreign living. Outwardly the principal hotel had a Western aspect, four stories high and looking out across the river and back across the town. But it was a typical Chinese hotel inside, with haphazard cooking going on in what we reserve as the hotel lobby, miserable narrow stairways unswept since Confucius first left home, gambling and the fondling of prostitutes going on openly. . . .

. . . I had trusted to luck to get along on the few words of mandarin that are similar to those of the Kwangtung dialect, with the added hope of running across some returned emigrant; and in the end I was not deceived. . . . It was almost dusk . . . when a pleasant fattish-looking youth in Western garb stepped up and introduced himself as 'Mr. Lee' and in almost the same breath volunteered the information that he was owner – with his family . . . of the Far Eastern Restaurant on Cleveland's once proud Euclid Avenue. . . . [. . .]

Mr. Lee and I were strolling about town next morning when we ran across an individual whom he introduced as 'Fred Hang.' He was an American, he lost no time in assuring me, born in Portland, Oregon, and recently graduated from one of its high schools. With a cloth cap pulled down over one eye, the latest college-man's-model coat and trousers sagging about his frame, low shoes, loud socks, and a speech as redolent of our streets as it was free from the slightest hint of a foreign accent, there was nothing whatever except the unconcealed eye to so much as hint that I had not run across an ordinary American high-school boy here in the heart of the Sze Yap. His relatives lived here, it seemed, and he had been back once as a 'kid,' and now he had come again, to get married. . . . Perhaps because it was the only genuine touch of America to be had in Kungyik, exiled Fred was hanging about the railroad station even on so eventful a day, one leg thrown in un-Chinese fashion over a rail and flanked by half a dozen awe-stricken small boys, a curiously incongruous figure among the swarming Chinese, with whom he could scarcely exchange a word. He didn't care for American girls, he confided . . . that is, as wives. They were 'too fast' and preferred play to work. What he wanted was one of these Chinese country school-girls, and his relatives had found him one. Yes, he 'liked Kungyik all right', but found it 'very lonesome'. He would stay a year or so and then go back, to study architecture in Washington State University. Would his wife go with him? 'Not on your life.' She would stay right here in Kungyik.

22) *The mistakes of China*
(Rodney Gilbert, *What's Wrong with China*, pp. 236–7)
Japan has had access to nothing in the Occident that was not free to China, but the same material and scientific assets which Japan has imported to her own great advantage, have simply provided China's evil genii with media of expression. The modern machinery of war, in the use of which the Chinese are too conceited to take proper instruction, is not used to maintain internal peace, nor to defend the nation's honour and territories, but has served more and more every year to break down authority and the respect for authority, has provided both bandits and uniformed hordes with means to loot and kill the unarmed farmers and traders, with the result that from one end of the country to the other commerce labours under such impositions

and at such risk that consumers both in China and abroad are unconsciously paying an enormously heavy insurance and a hundred different kinds of taxes which appear upon no government financial statement.

Communications are so abused that they contribute much more to the impoverishment and confusion of the country than to its wealth. To modernize industry in any part of China but the communities under foreign control is to make one's business conspicuous and therefore to invite official attentions which mean extinction for any enterprise that is not capitalized by powerful officials and therefore protected by them. Western ideas in politics are reduced to slogans and shibboleths which simply serve as apologies for official outrages against the public good. The new political creeds and 'isms' of the West act upon the Chinese mind as the loco weed acts upon the otherwise well-behaved pony. . . . Such propaganda as the Soviet agents have been bringing into China during the past five years is responsible for more wild and incoherent thinking and talking, more confusion in the State, and more loss of national prestige than Moscow could hope to inspire in any Occidental country in a half-century. China's future has been much more seriously prejudiced by the ideas imported and peddled by such persons as Bertrand Russell, John Dewey, Tagore and Karakhan, than by all the opium, morphia, heroin, cocaine and hashish imported or produced in China during the past three centuries.

23) *The student movement*
(Paul Monroe, *China: A Nation in Evolution*, pp. 284–6)
The three outstanding factors in the Chinese situation to-day are the militarists, the nationalists, and the students. Not so powerful as the militarists, yet – since they represent a reconstruction force as well as one of political agitation – of far greater ultimate significance, is the student body. Perhaps no question regarding China is more frequently asked by the American public than an explanation of the student influence. [. . .]

The scholar of the past took many years in the making. . . . Scholars were products of extended study and reflection, and of experience in subordinate positions of authority, rather than trained products of schools. That the present student is an immature youth, drawn from his home and association with elders and thrown into dormitories where he associates with youths only, has made but slight diminution in his influence and repute. But this situation has made a great difference in the instability and emotionalism of student opinion, and in its susceptibility to the influence of mob psychology.

Some features of student life to-day will further explain their political interest and influence. Most of the middle schools and colleges of China are situated in the provincial capitals. In many of these capital cities twenty to thirty thousand students are congregated. They live in crowded dormitories, with few comforts, little better than emergency barracks. Teachers and administrators have little contact with their students, even in the classroom. For the most part teachers have little influence over the students. These latter are young when they leave home – thirteen to fifteen years of age. Perhaps the median age of this great student body is not over seventeen years. On the other hand, there are numerous students who are mature and who exercise great influence. It is sometimes said that the student movement is headed and maintained by a handful of students (usually extremists) in each student center. That conditions are ideal for the control of mass psychology and for developing such radical leadership is undoubtedly true. This sometimes occurs. But it would be a great misinterpretation of the situation not to recognize the genuine patriotic, political interest of the student body, no matter how immature; and the devotion and disinterested, even if sometimes unwise, leadership of these selected leaders.

24) *The Chinese have a right*

(O.D. Rasmussen, *What's Right with China*, pp. xv–xvi)

When women of the Yangtze valley clamor against polygamy, infant engagement, obsolete divorce restrictions; when students clamor against 'imperialism,' exploitation, and obsolete foreign privileges; when modern intellectuals clamor against foreign control of their tariffs, extraterritoriality, and nonrepresentation in concession governments, they are all imbued with the same spirit of nationalism; they are all clamoring for the one basic abstract principle of freedom and justice. [...]

Earned or unearned, deserved or undeserved, the Chinese have a right to clamor for the abolition of whatever, in their minds, throttles their national growth; they have a right to clamor for sovereignty over the treaty ports which stand as gigantic alien sentinels at the gates to the trading wealth of China. They have a right to clamor for tariff autonomy as part of the basic power of government; they have a right to clamor for the abolition of a host of little independent 'kingdoms' whose acquired rights of 'neutrality,' apart from anything else, are a denial of sovereign rights and privileges. The Chinese have been unable to make any move toward rehabilitation without stepping on neutral and alien rights. At every turn they meet with some manifestation of vested foreign interests. They are hemmed in by countless spheres of interest, treaty terms and obligations, all bristling with penalties for deliberate or accidental breaches of observance. They are not masters in their own house; not even to the extent of punishing their own wrongdoers who have gained 'political asylum' in 'neutral' foreign concessions.

25) *Present condition of prostitution in Peking*
(S.D. Gamble, *Peking: A Social Survey*, pp. 249–51)
To one at all familiar with conditions of vice in the large cities of America, a visit to the red light district in Peking brings a distinct surprise. Instead of finding a place where the rougher elements of the community meet – a center of carousing, disorder, and drunkenness – one finds order, quietness and discipline.

The buildings are not allowed to have any windows or porches facing the street, so there is no open display. The entrances, however, are marked with electrically lighted lanterns and with the name and class of the house. During the evening the girls' names, written on brass or wood tablets or embroidered on silk, are hung outside the doors of the first and second class houses.

. . . A visitor is always announced by one of the servants and is usually met by the proprietor or mistress of the house. He is then invited into one of the rooms and asked whether he knows any one in the house whom he would like to call in. If not, he is asked whether he would like to see the girls and all the inmates of the house are called. They come to the door, one by one, bow, stand for a second, and then pass on. In the second class houses the girls are called by number; in the first class houses, by name. [. . .]

The character, age and appearance of the women naturally vary with the class of the brothel in which they are living. In the third and fourth class houses the women for the most part are between 20 and 30 years old, are rather ignorant and gross in appearance and are dressed in ordinary Chinese clothes made from cheap Chinese blue cotton cloth. On the other hand the women in the first and second class houses, particularly those in the first class, are attractive and even striking in appearance, are dressed in beautiful silks, many of them well versed in the arts of entertaining, having been given a careful course of preparation for many years, while some have even had a good education. Most of the girls in the first class houses are between 16 and 18 years old and it is said that none of them are over 20.

Although extremely modest in behavior, the girls do not seem at all shamefaced but are dignified and self-controlled in manner. Many of their faces, however, are marked by the nervous strain and tension of their extremely strenuous life of social entertainment.

26) *The fuel problem*
(F.H. King, *Farmers of Forty Centuries*, p. 123)
With the vast and ever increasing demands made upon the products of cultivated fields, for food, for apparel, for furnishings and for cordage, better soil management must grow more important as populations multiply. With the increasing cost and ultimate exhaustion of mineral fuel; with our timber vanishing rapidly . . . the time must surely come when, in short period rotations, there will be grown upon the farm materials from which to manufacture not only paper and the substitutes for lumber, but fuels as well. . . .

When these statements were made in 1905 we did not know that for centuries there had existed in China, Korea and Japan a density of population such as to require the extensive cultivation of crops for fuel and building material, as well as for fabrics, by the ordinary methods of tillage, and hence another of the many surprises we had was the solution these people had reached of their fuel problem. Their solution is direct and the simplest possible. Dress to make fuel for warmth of body unnecessary, and burn the coarser stems of crops, such as cannot be eaten, or employed to feed animals or otherwise made useful.

27) *Chinese and American farms compared*
(John Lossing Buck, *Chinese Farm Economy*, pp. 422–3)
The basis of Chinese agriculture is a farm system of unfenced scattered plots of land for the most part inherited, difficult of management from

the farmsteads which are usually located in villages or hamlets of varying size. These villages and hamlets dot the landscape about as thickly as do the solitary farmsteads in the United States, and this signifies a dense population as well as a rural social system entirely different from that in most western countries.

The area per farm, while small, is not as small as it first appears, because much of the land produces two crops a year and the crops are all food or fiber crops for direct human utilization. . . .

The farm land is generally worked by owners, although approximately one-fifth is farmed by tenants and another one-fifth by part owners, the extent of tenancy varying from almost none to nearly one hundred per cent tenants in some localities. Systems of rent are quite similar to those found in other countries. Rental charges, however, are often not fair either for the tenant or the landlord and on the average rents should be reduced something over one-fifth the present amount.

Not only is the area of land worked by the farmer in China small, but he has also far smaller capital and equipment than the western farmer. In fact, his main investment is labor, but even this is not very great since the Chinese farm averages only two men giving full time to the farm business compared with approximately one and one-half men in the United States. . . .

The production from the farm business in China and in the United States is remarkably equal in quantity per unit of land, although the method of obtaining these products [is] entirely different. In the United States the chief means has been the use of capital as well as labor; in China it has been by the use of labor, for the most part human labor, and with very little capital. The resulting production per unit of labor in the United States is apparently at least twenty-five fold greater than in China.

28) *Forms of recreation in a south China village*
(D.H. Kulp, *Country Life in South China*, pp. 281–3)
. . . Traditionally, play is taboo, but practically, it is allowed for children and engaged in by adults. Not all forms of play are equally good but none are punishable, not even those kinds tacitly disapproved of by the better members of the community because of their bad effects.

Following is a list of the forms of recreation engaged in by children (girls' games are starred*): The more active forms of play are: Swimming, running races, wrestling and boxing, hopping and skipping*, rowing boats, frog race, catch the monkey, foot and inch or 'striking the ear', shuttlecock*, throwing a ball*, blind man's buff*, rolling a coin, flying kites, archery (very rare).

The less strenuous forms are: Fishing, fish fighting, cricket fighting, hunting in a minor way, marbles, keeping domestic animals, catching frogs, catching wild bees, wasps and insects, imitating activities of adults or of theatrical performances, practicing music, reading stories or novels, singing dramatic songs, making and using whistles, telling and listening to stories, feasting, watching theatrical performances, gambling, calling to spirits or ghosts . . . , jacks*.

The adult forms of recreation are: Fishing, hunting, boxing, gambling, feasting, attending theatrical performances, playing musical instruments and singing, reading stories and novels, listening to stories and novels, telling stories, smoking (tobacco and opium), gossip and debate, idling. [. . .]

The forms of recreation for women are very few. The women watch theatricals, listen to readings, music, watch the religious processions or participate in other ceremonies that provide a recreative aspect because of their infrequency, such as weddings, funerals, ancestral worship, and the like. They also embroider, occasionally paint, but generally gossip. In the larger homes, some of the women care for flowers, water-lilies and goldfish. Time hangs heavily on their hands.

The greatest single improvement in village recreation that could be introduced would be radio, but broadcasting is not yet established in Swatow.

29) *On the first sighting of Peking Man*
(L.H. Dudley Buxton, *China: The Land and People*, pp. 41–2)
Meanwhile in China itself [Davidson Black] believes that he has found the remains of an 'archaic hominid'. Some years ago Schlosser found a tooth in a Chinese drug store, for the Chinese set great store on fossils as medicine. He suggested that it might be of Tertiary date, and described it as being a molar tooth of *Homo* ? or *Anthropoid* ? *gen. sp. undetermined*. Since that time certain teeth were found at Choukoutien,

south-west of Peking. . . . In this case there is no doubt as to the deposit from which the specimens came, and Black's specimen, to which special attention should be directed, was seen *in situ*. . . . Black concludes that the teeth belong to two individuals, a child and an adult, and the species has been named *Sinanthropus pekinensis*. I have only seen photographs and drawings of the specimens. . . . In view, however, of the fact that even so experienced a palaeontologist as W.K. Gregory was deceived into thinking that the tooth of a pig was that of an anthropoid, *Hesperopithecus*, I do not feel in a position to express a definite opinion. A witty writer in *The Times* suggested that possibly the spirit of *Hesperopithecus* may be regarding the old gods sadly from the branches of a monkey-puzzle tree. It is to be hoped that a neighbouring branch is not being prepared by some industrious Taoist spirit for *Sinanthropus*.

30) *The Caves of the Thousand Buddhas*
(Langdon Warner, *The Long Old Road in China*, pp. 213–19)
It was veritably Chien Fo Tung, the Caves of the Thousand Buddhas, for, big and little, half-obliterated or almost perfect, there were tens of thousands of figures on those walls. Many of the most superb were so nearly gone that one must stand at a distant and discreet angle to know that they were there at all. They seemed to be retiring gradually from the light of common day. . . .

But it was with a shock that I traced, on the oval faces and calm mouths, the foul scratches of Slavic obscenity and the regimental numbers which Ivan and his *polk* had left there. Two years before, a little group of four hundred Russian soldiers . . . pursued by the Red armies, had fled through Turkestan. . . . [. . .]

Obviously, some specimens of these paintings must be secured for study at home, and, more important still, for safe-keeping against further vandalism. I had been revolving the subject in my mind for months. The Germans and the British had attacked frescoed mud walls from the rear and had been able to cut out and preserve important sections of decorated surface. But caves hollowed from the very bowels of the stone cliffs were not so easy a problem. [. . .]

Before leaving Peking I had provided myself with a quantity of the fixative recommended by the chemists to tie together the ancient pigment, now as delicate and easily dislodged as chalk dust on a blackboard. Also I had with me the ingredients for the soluble bed which must be applied to the painting after the colour was judged secure.

Being neither chemist nor trained picture restorer, but an ordinary person with an active archaeological conscience, what I was about to do seemed both sacrilegious and impossible. [. . .]

Without touching the sixth-century work, of which no other example is known to exist, and avoiding the greatest masterpieces of the Tang period, I chose some Tang figures which were left in fair condition from partly-destroyed groups. Though far from being the most important in the place, these would prove treasures the like of which we had never seen in America, and which even Berlin, with its wealth of frescoes sawn in squares from the stucco walls of Turkestan, might envy.

Five days of labour from morning till dark and five nights of remorse for what I had done and of black despair, conquered with difficulty each morning, saw the fragments of paintings securely packed in felts and lashed tightly between flat boards, ready for the eighteen-weeks' trip by springless jolting cart, railroad, and ship to the Fogg Museum at Harvard.

THE NATIONALIST
REVOLUTION AND THE
NANKING DECADE

The Nationalist Revolution of 1926–8 can be traced to the 'May 30th Incident' in Shanghai in 1925, and to the burst of nationalist feeling which then swept China (1). Meyrick Hewlett, the British consul at the port of Amoy, described events there in response to that incident (2). H.G.W. Woodhead, the editor of *The China Year Book*, sought to excuse one of the most notorious examples of foreign imperialism, the exclusion of Chinese from the public gardens in the Shanghai International Settlement (3).

The Northern Expedition, which started in July 1926, brought Nationalist forces into the Yangtze valley and raised the possibilities of class war and of a threat to the interests of the western powers. Dramatic events took place in Wuhan, the triple city on the Yangtze comprising Hankow, Hanyang and Wuchang, where the 1911 revolution had started. Tom Mann, a British trade-union leader and a Communist described the upsurge of trade union activity in that area (4). H. Owen Chapman, a doctor working in Hankow, in May 1927 recorded a scandalous affair connected with the emancipation of women (5). Vincent Sheean, who had several interviews with Borodin, the Comintern representative, placed the Chinese revolution in a world perspective (6). Before the end of the year the tide had turned against the radical wing of the Nationalist movement. The liquidation of the Communists in Shanghai was described by John Powell, an American journalist (7). One of the most famous novels set in China, André Malraux's *Man's Fate*, took as its subject this suppression of the left. Malraux rejected the view, held by so many westerners in the past, that China was a world separate from, and contradictory to, the West. Instead he insisted on the common nature of man's struggle (8).

The years from 1928 to 1937 are known as the Nanking decade, the period when the Nationalist government, having reunited China and having moved the capital to Nanking, sought, with a mixed degree of success, to implement a policy of modernization. For one observer China's democratic future was assured now that it was in the hands of graduates of American universities, many of whom were converts to Christianity (9). Others saw the many problems still to be tackled, for example the major famine in the north, reported by L.C. Arlington, who worked for the China International Famine Relief Commission (10). After 1927 the Communists in their rural bases were a thorn in the side of the Nationalists, though J.O.P. Bland, who had worked in China since 1883, was dismissive of their chances of succeeding (11). The adventurous British journalist Peter Fleming was less sceptical. Having tried in vain to reach the Communists' base in Kiangsi, he obtained an unexpected interview with Chiang Kai-shek, their chief opponent (12). The one westerner who had a detailed knowledge of what was going on in the Communist-held areas was the Comintern agent Otto Braun. His version of the origins of the Long March in 1934 contradicted the explanation put forward by Mao Tse-tung (13).

It was in this decade that westerners made the first detailed surveys of conditions in the countryside. Gerald Winfield was convinced that the starting point for China's modernization had to be sanitation. His research into fecal-borne disease led him to make horrifying estimates of the infestation by worms of the Chinese population (14). A more attractive view of rural China was presented in Pearl Buck's novel *The Good Earth*, first published in 1931, which became the best-selling western book about China of all time. In it she described the peasants as leading lives which were honest, hard-working and ultimately satisfying (15). Olga Lang studied the Chinese family, and showed it undergoing significant changes, for example in its recognition of romantic love (16).

Some writers were critical of the Nationalists. The American journalist Agnes Smedley rejected any idealization of the past and attached herself to radical opponents of the government. Her circle of acquaintances included the novelist Lu Hsün (17). R.H. Tawney, who visited China in 1931, noted the continued use of child labour (18).

Other westerners who lived in China during the Nanking decade were more optimistic: Ruth Hemenway, an American medical missionary, wrote hopefully about the New Life Movement which she encountered in Kiangsi in 1936 (19).

Some writers were more concerned with cultural matters. Harold Acton noted the response of students at Peking National University to his lectures on English literature (20). L.C Arlington and William Lewisohn, writing in 1933, were already expressing concern over the destruction of old Peking (21). The most evocative description of Peking can be found in *The Years that were Fat* by George Kates, who lived there from 1933 to 1941. J.K. Fairbank, introducing the paperback edition of the book, wrote 'What Kates describes cannot be found today' (22). A more practical note was sounded by Carl Crow, an American advertising agent who presented a good-humoured and essentially optimistic view of China's commercial progress during this period (23).

1) *The 30 May Atrocious Incident*
(Putnam Weale, *Why China Sees Red*, pp. 19–24)
... It was not entirely the domineering attitude of Japanese overseers which had discredited the Japanese factories and made them the centres of increasing disturbance. An unseen hand was undoubtedly directing a movement which was far more political than industrial. . . .
It is significant that on May 7th the Peking student bodies . . . had suddenly decided to hold a giant demonstration on Humiliation Day, as the anniversary of the filing of the Japanese ultimatum of 1915 over the Twenty-One Demands is called. . . .
The National University of Peking, dreaming perhaps of becoming another Smolny Institute, sent instructions to other student bodies to use the case of the killing of a Chinese workman in a Japanese mill in Shanghai, which had already led to a strike, as an excuse for attacking the whole position of foreign interests in China, Shanghai being marked down as the most favourable battle-field on which to wage a war without weapons.
May 30th was a Saturday, and Saturday in a community dominated by English ideals is a day of sport. Only for Europeans, however, and not for the swarming crowds of a city that with its suburbs already possesses nearly two million inhabitants. . . . Watching over this great community was a small force of 4000 police, three-quarters of whom were Chinese. [. . .]

According to the evidence in the only court that has sat on the case, the Shanghai Mixed Court, this is the exact sequence of events.

At 12.40 on this particular day a general warning was telephoned to all police stations in the foreign settlement that student demonstrations were imminent. . . . An hour later, at 1.55, to be precise, the inspector in charge of the Nanking Road district, which is the equivalent of Regent Street in London or Fifth Avenue in New York, where thousands can collect as by the waving of a wand, was notified that public speaking had commenced and that students were collecting in small crowds with flags in their hands. Single-handed and ignorant of what lay behind, the inspector proceeded to work precisely as laid down by instructions. Arrested students, when they were formally charged, admitted that they had no permits to speak on the streets, but denied the authority of the Council to restrain them from patriotic actions. Disorderly scenes began to occur, and it was not long before isolated European police were fighting for their lives. The rapidly growing crowd, incited by handbills and by paid agitators who appeared as if by magic, made the prospect more and more uninviting. By 3 o'clock in the afternoon the die was cast: but the evidence at the Police Court trial is silent as to what communications passed between police headquarters and the station which was confronted by these developments.

The fact that, twenty years before, this now historic Louza Police Station had been attacked and burnt by a mob no doubt dictated the next move. The inspector, abandoned to his own resources but determined not to lose control, fell back from the main thoroughfare, after having ordered all reserve police, Indian and Chinese, to load their carbines. The last act took place with that curious irrelevance which is always a characteristic of things prepared by an unkind fate. As the crowd surged forward, roaring with rage and ignorant of what was about to happen, a warning, which was never heard, was shouted. Then two sharp volleys were heard, forty-four shots in all, ushering in a period which will never see China the same.

2) *An anti-British demonstration in Amoy*
(Sir Meyrick Hewlett, *Forty Years in China*, p. 155)
I crossed the harbour early on the morning of 6th June 1925, about an hour before the time I had been told the demonstration was to take

place. After a chat with a Colonel Lin, who was in charge of the troops, I went to the offices of Messrs. Butterfield and Swire. It was not long before the procession came. It was headed by young fellows in firemen's helmets, short-sleeved dark shirts, shorts, black stockings and black shoes. They carried red-and-white pennons on lances and were picturesque enough if one's mind had not been fixed on matters weightier than a pleasing spectacle. The procession proper was composed of scholars, boys and girls, down to tiny mites of very young age. They were accompanied by riff-raff out for mischief. Headed by Shanghai agitators they yelled slogans: 'Annihilate the Imperialists', 'Abolish Consuls', 'Give us back the Concessions', 'Britons have slain our compatriots in Shanghai', 'Remember China's shame'. These slogans were also written on flags which had been smeared in blood. . . . I can remember feeling intense sorrow at watching children passing, shouting hatred and realising an age was being inaugurated with revenge and hatred as guiding principles.

3) *'Chinese and dogs are not admitted'*
(H.G.W. Woodhead, *The Truth About the Chinese Republic*, pp. 238–9)
I may refer here to a complaint which is frequently voiced by Chinese extremists regarding the exclusion of Chinese from the public gardens and recreation grounds. The statement is often made that outside the Public Gardens at Shanghai is a notice reading 'Chinese and dogs are not admitted.' This is not true, and never has been true. There is, it is true, a series of regulations, in English and Chinese, which prohibit Chinese in one case, and dogs in another, from entering the gardens. But they are separate regulations, and there has never been any suggestion that Chinese and dogs are classed together. When it is argued that the Chinese are affronted by such exclusion it is well to bear in mind one or two important considerations. First, there is the fact that the Public Gardens and Recreation Grounds were originally laid out by the foreign communities for their own use. They no more than suffice for the needs of the foreign residents, who would be crowded out if they were thrown open freely to the Chinese.

Secondly, they constitute the only open spaces to which foreign children can be sent with safety. Infectious and contagious diseases are rife in China. It is conservatively estimated that thirty per cent. of the entire population suffers from trachoma, while scarlet fever, typhus, small-pox, and other diseases are frequently raging in the Chinese cities, where no attempt to control or isolate them is made. It is, therefore, self-preservation, rather than racial prejudice that leads to the exclusion of Chinese from the open spaces which foreigners have laid out for their own enjoyment.

4) *A fever of expectation*
(Tom Mann, *"What I Saw in China"*, pp. 22–3)

Our train left Hankow shortly before midnight on April 19th. It was truly a memorable night and day for the delegates as well as for all other passengers on that train. At every station, without a single exception, all along the line, all through the night and the following day, the delegation were greeted by masses of peasants and workers, who crowded the platforms with banners and bands. Every hour or so we were roused by a distant discharge of fire-crackers that made the neighbourhood rattle. This was the signal to us that we were approaching a station, and that we were ex-pected to come out and address the crowds which came to greet us. For over twenty-four hours we were, so to speak, in a fever of expectation. . . .

We divided our comrades into shifts, each one taking a turn at speaking, while the others attempted to rest. Torrents of rain poured down all through the night and the following day. But as we progressed the crowds at the stations became larger and larger. [. . .]

At about six o'clock in the afternoon we reached the station at Milo, where a mass meeting with 5,000 people was held. There we learned that reaction is still running high in that neighbourhood. The peasants are suffering untold misery under the rule of the gentry. The Kuomintang has not yet been organised in this town. The trade unions are in the preparatory stage. Some 70 peasants' groups (not yet Peasants' Union) are already in existence, but they are still very weak.

We arrived in Changsha shortly before midnight of April 20th. We were met by many thousands of people who had been waiting for over ten hours at the station. . . .

The People's Club

With music and cheers and revolutionary songs and slogans resounding through the night and arousing the entire city, a long procession through the town brought us to our quarters, the former Y.M.C.A. building.

This was the first symptom of significant and deep-going changes that had already taken place in Hunan. What was formerly the Y.M.C.A. is now *'The People's Club'*. What was formerly a modern and very clever distillery of 'Americanisation' and a camouflaged channel for the penetration of American imperialism under the cloak of Christianity and Y.M.C.A. philanthropy is now a centre of recreation for the Chinese workers and peasants and students. This People's Club, a modern, splendidly kept building... resembles very much some of the 'People's Clubs' and 'Workers' Clubs' in Soviet Russia.

5) *The Naked Women's Parade*
(H. Owen Chapman, *The Chinese Revolution 1926–27*, pp. 86–7)
... The doctrine of 'free love' as propagated in Russia in the early years of the Revolution of 1917 was now widely preached in Hankow, to the utter disgust of the great bulk of the steady citizens. In some of the propagandist schools, where students of both sexes were in training, men and women slept in the same dormitories, and there seems little doubt but that the doctrine of the 'common wife' . . . , fell on willing ears. After all, it is a rigidly logical though extreme extension of the Communist doctrine.

Of all the extravagances of sexual bravado that which attracted the greatest notice was the Naked Women's Parade. The particulars were first published early in April, calling for applications from women willing to participate in a naked parade through the Hankow streets on 1st May. Only women of perfect physique were eligible, and proponents were to undergo a physical examination on application. The purpose of the parade was to make a passionate and defiant gesture in an arresting way, asserting woman's right to conduct herself entirely as she chose without let or hindrance from anyone. The news created a great sensation in Hankow, most Chinese receiving it with the gravest misgiving and with vicarious shame. Reporters were sent up from Shanghai to make inquiries: the world was waiting to see whether in this feature too the Government would precisely follow the Russian precedent of a few years ago. The parade never took place. On 2nd May, after the whole of Hankow had been talking of it for a month, three Chinese were arrested and punished for 'maliciously spreading a false rumour' that such a parade was to take place; and the next day the Hupeh Women's Union published a denial that there was any intention of holding the parade, and the Government organ (*The People's Tribune*) poured the greatest scorn on the whole 'fabrication.' But as the newspaper itself admits that for several weeks it had been inundated with inquiries about the Parade, how comes it that it waited until two days after the date fixed for it to deny what was the talk of the whole people? Everything points to the explanation that the Nationalist Government, fearing to face the world-wide scandal that they rather tardily realised would result, cancelled the fixture at the last moment.

6) *The revolutionary spirit in Hankow*
(Vincent Sheean, *Personal History*, pp. 226–7)
... [Borodin] exemplified in his own person, and pointed out in the phenomena around him, the peculiar qualities of intellectual consistency, social philosophy, selflessness and determination that combine to form something I have called ... the revolutionary spirit.

That spirit was abroad in Hankow from the time the Cantonese armies entered the city until the collapse of the revolutionary government on July 5th. It was to be seen in Chinese and Russians, Left Kuomintang organizers and Communists, workmen, students and agitators – not in all of them, of course, but in a large enough number to confirm the existence of something new in the confusion of China. There were Communist students, sometimes of rich families, who became coolies so as to be able to organize the coolies for revolution. There were educated Chinese girls who risked death in the effort to tell the workers and peasants who their real enemies were. One of these girls – we all knew her in Hankow – was disembowelled by Chiang Kai-shek's soldiers on June 21st in Hangchow for saying that the Nanking war lord did not represent the party or principles of Sun Yat-sen. Her intestines were taken out and wrapped around her body while she was still alive. ... The horrors of the counter-revolution were not unexpected: these young Chinese knew what awaited them and went ahead just the same. The impulse that made them offer their lives for the cause was not a suicidal, neurotic yearning for Nirvana, as it might have been in similar crises in India or Japan. Such varieties of mystic ardour were . . . unknown to China. The Chinese operated on a colder and purer conviction, the belief that courageous sacrifice in the service of an idea was the best means of propagating that idea. The individual was, as so often in China, sacrificed to the race, and the young men and girls died for generations unborn.

7) *The Blue-Green Society*
(J.B. Powell, *My Twenty-Five Years in China*, pp. 151–5)
Bearing in mind the fact that Shanghai is China's 'key' city . . . it was obvious that both groups in the Kuomintang had made preparations to seize control of the Chinese-administered sections of the city. Propaganda squads attached to the radical branch of the party were first on the scene and had completely undermined the morale of the Northern troops . . . they evacuated before the Southerners were within a hundred miles of the city. . . .

The Communists thus had an opportunity to make their preparations. There was no questioning the fact that prevailing sentiment among the student and labor groups favored the leftists and their program of social reform. Preparations had been made for seizure of control of Shanghai in the manner of Hankow, and, as at Hankow, there were parades, mass meetings, speeches, and distribution of literature. The walls of buildings were plastered with posters denouncing foreign imperialists. Any Chinese who helped a foreigner was designated in word and cartoon as a 'running-dog' of the foreign imperialists. [. . .]

Out of the confusion then prevailing in Shanghai there emerged a figure, previously unknown, who took on the composite character of an earlier-decade American gangster and political boss. The character was Dou Yu-seng, now listed in the respectable China 'Who's Who' as a 'banker, philanthropist, and welfare worker'. . . .

Dou Yu-seng started his career in the Shanghai French Concession as a youthful fruit peddler. He soon discovered the places where opium was sold illicitly, and familiarized himself with the racketeering, hijacking, and other practices which prevailed in Shanghai. . . . In his rise to power Dou solved a local political problem which previously had defied solution: he amalgamated two powerful secret political organizations whose activities extended far back into the era of the Manchu

Dynasty. The organizations, known as the Blue Society and Green Society, originally were engaged in intrigue against the Manchus, but after the creation of the Republic they degenerated into gangster-ism.... Dou Yu-seng ... became head of the rejuvenated organization known as the Blue-Green Society, which performed functions, according to Chinese lights, probably not greatly different from those performed by political groups which dominate the large cities of the United States.[...]

Political conditions in the French Concession facilitated Dou's rise to power. The Shanghai French Concession ... was governed not directly from Paris, but second-hand through Hanoi.... The ineffi-ciency and corruption which prevailed in the French Colony were repeated in the French Concession....

Dou Yu-seng and his associates took advantage of this situation and became the real controllers of the French Concession. Dou ruled his empire from his home in the Concession, which resembled an arsenal. But he was a liberal contributor to charities and he came to hold more chairmanships on directorates of Chinese banks and business houses than any other man in the city. His orders were enforced by hundreds of armed guards, popularly known as 'Dou's plain-clothes men.'

When conditions became chaotic after the withdrawal of the Northern troops, Dou Yu-seng stepped into the breach and notified the local foreign authorities that he would assume responsibility for the maintenance of law and order, pending the arrival of the Nationalist troops. It was at this point that the shooting began; it continued without intermission for many days. Preparations which the radicals and Communists had made for seizing the city back-fired, and the reign of terror which the Reds had planned was turned against them.

No accurate count was made of bodies which littered the streets of the native areas, but Edgar Snow ... estimated that more than 5,000 leftists were killed. According to Snow's account, Chou En-lai, the Communist leader, had organized 600,000 workers who staged a general strike, completely tying up the industries of the city.... A so-called 'citizens' government' was proclaimed, stated Snow's account.

But the Communist coup was short-lived. It could not stand up against the experienced gunmen of Dou Yu-seng. When the Nation-alist troops ... arrived at Shanghai they found the job already completed; the city was handed over to them by Dou Yu-seng and his lieutenants. Chou En-lai, the Communist leader, was imprisoned and other radical leaders, who were not captured and executed, fled to Hankow.

8) *Hankow, 1927*
(André Malraux, *Man's Fate*, p. 167)
The peace of the night once more. Not a siren, nothing but the lapping of the water. Along the banks, near the street-lamps crackling with insects, coolies lay sleeping in postures of people afflicted with the plague. Here and there, little round red posters; on them was figured a single character: HUNGER. He felt ... that on this very night, in all China, and throughout the West, including half of Europe, men were hesitating as he was, torn by the same torment between their discipline and the massacre of their own kind. Those stevedores who were protesting did not understand. But, even when one understood, how choose the sacrifice, here, in this city to which the West looked for the destiny of four hundred million men and perhaps its own, and which was sleeping on the edge of the river in the uneasy sleep of the famished – in impotence, in wretchedness, in hatred?

9) *Thronged with the graduates of American colleges*
(A.N. Holcombe, *The Spirit of the Chinese Revolution*, pp. 3–5)
... Sun Yat-sen ... received his education in American and English schools and colleges. He married for his second wife a graduate of an American woman's college. He sent his son to the University of California. ... Chiang Kai-shek was not educated in America, nor has he, to my knowledge, ever professed Christianity, but his wife is a Christian and a graduate of Wellesley College. They were married by the head of the Chinese Y.M.C.A. and for a beverage he drinks unfermented grape juice. ... Both T.V. Soong and C.T. Wang are American college graduates. Wang studied at the University of Michigan and at Yale. ... Soong studied at Vanderbilt University and at Harvard, where he graduated in 1915, having specialized in economics. I have looked up his record at the college office, and while I will betray no academic secrets, I will say that his record affords no comfort to those who pretend that high academic rank bodes ill for future distinction. I lunched one day in Mr. Soong's office at the

Ministry of Finance in Nanking, together with the other Harvard men who held office in the Nationalist Government at that time. All the principal bureau chiefs in the Ministry of Finance were Harvard graduates, and I could not help but feel that the prestige of Harvard was at stake in their conduct of the national finances. Besides Harvard and Yale, Columbia, Cornell, Oberlin, and the University of California were represented among the principal department heads at Nanking. . . .

10) *Famine in Shensi*
(L.C. Arlington, *Through the Dragon's Eyes*, pp. 245–7, 249–50)
What I witnessed really beggars description. In the I-ch'uan district alone no less than 830 villages were affected. I hardly saw one able-bodied man; they were either dead, or had joined the army, or had become brigands, leaving the fields untilled. The villages were full of children, boys and girls between the ages of four and ten; no young women were to be seen, most of them having been kidnapped by brigands, while some had been sold or had committed suicide. In one hamlet I visited, originally containing some 500 inhabitants, there were but 100 persons left, 200 or more having died from starvation, or from typhus brought on by louse bites. Many men had departed for regions unknown, leaving everything behind them – wives, children and all earthly belongings. In one hovel I saw several old folks lying ill in bed with rags for covering; in another hovel two only were left out of a family of ten, while the clothing of the eight dead was piled up against the walls of the room, looking for all the world like so many dummies awaiting burial. . . . Many, yea, scores, of the villages were in ruins; the mud hovels had all tumbled down because the wooden beams, door sills, etc., had been used for fuel. Not a few sufferers were existing on the seeds of the *Huai Shu* (*Saphora*), mostly used for making yellow dye and as a haemorrhoidal cure. These seeds and blossoms were simply soaked in cold water – there being no fuel left to cook them – and when well swollen they were devoured with great gusto. Every one of these people had a deadly, ghostly pallor. . . .

We tried our best to get grain into the most distressed areas, but it was difficult; hundreds of tons remained held up on the way for months. The communications were wretched, heavy rain stopped transport for days, and there were also the military movements, which, rightly or wrongly, claimed right of way. What with gross procrastination and supineness on the part of the Chinese, who made all sorts of empty promises of help, our progress was exceedingly slow – so slow, in fact, that one felt like giving up in despair. Yet common humanity demanded that we should do our best. So we proceeded with our first task – building and repair of roads – which we followed up with irrigation measures to give the people work and food. The crops appeared excellent . . . right up to the edge of the worst famine district. Alas! opium, too, was grown in considerable quantity. . . . As the American delegates of the Red Cross expedition truly remarked, much of the famine trouble here is of an artificial origin, arising from the warring factions, bandits, ex-soldiers etc. Yet a great deal of it is also due to natural causes, shortage of rain, and so on. [. . .]

The attempt of the China International Famine Relief Commission to undertake any sort of work in Shensi at present, as it seems to me, is futile. Large sums contributed by both the Chinese and Americans are merely wasted. Corruption – even amongst the staff employed by the Relief Committee – interference by the military, banditry, opium-growing, general inefficiency, large overhead expenses, and the bungling attempts to distribute funds and grain are all responsible for this waste.

11) *Is there a Red Peril in China?*
(J.O.P. Bland, *China: The Pity of It*, pp. 282–4)
The movement itself, the forces behind it, and the phenomena which it produces, represent, in fact, ideas and objectives wholly different from those commonly implied by the word Communism; in no part of China does there exist a force of opinion capable of creating the type of social organisation produced in Europe by the economic doctrines of Karl Marx or the political principles of Lenin. The Socialist ideas propounded in Sun Yat-sen's 'Three Principles' were, like his conversion to Christianity, an imported *'article d'occasion,'*. . . . The principles which determine the workings of a revolutionary or rebellious movement remain unchanged. Behind them lie the two paramount instincts of Chinese social life, i.e., the desire for posterity and that of family enrichment at the expense of other families. The two Chinese characters usually displayed on the banners of the 'Red' armies mean, in plain English, 'Divide Property,' an economic doctrine which has

appealed to landless and lawless members of every community from time immemorial; but the idea of a division of property for the benefit of the community, and not of the individual, is one which could never enter the Chinese mind. Every Chinese of the 'have-nots' Class, every desperate victim of the present anarchy, is a 'Communist,' in the sense that he is ready to support any faction which promises him a chance of transferring other people's property to himself, and the landless survivors of civil war, flood and famine are naturally disposed to support a 'Revolution for the protection of land.' But their conception of Communistic principles begins and ends with the individual and the family. [...]

The 'Red Peril' is real enough in China to-day, and it will continue to make life a burden and a terror to millions, until, in Heaven's good time, benevolent despotism in the hands of a strong ruler shall have restored China's ancient ways of stability. But the 'Red Peril' with which the Kuomintang propagandists would make our flesh creep, the vision of China's 400 millions organised to Communism for Russia's purposes of world-revolution, may be dismissed as impossible. . . .

12) *Chiang Kai-shek*
(Peter Fleming, *One's Company*, p. 227)

As a rule, contact with the great brings out the worst in me. The more exalted a man's position, the less impressionable I become. . . .

But before Chiang Kai-shek I retired abashed. Here was a man with a presence, with that something incalculable to him to which the herd instinctively defers. He was strong and silent by nature, not by artifice. . . . He may not be a great statesman, or a very great soldier; events may prove that the best that can be said of him is that he has been the effective head of the best government China has had since the Revolution – a government, incidentally, which is older by several years than any now holding office in the West. But at any rate Chiang Kai-shek has something to him. He is a personality in his own right. He is not only not a mediocrity or a wind-bag, but he could never look like one. That, I think, entitles him to a certain singularity among modern political leaders.

13) *On the origins of the Long March*
(Otto Braun, *A Comintern Agent in China 1932-1939*, pp. 81–4)

According to my notes from 1939, which were based on 1934 estimates of the Red Army General Headquarters . . . the Central

Army Group's actual strength at the time of departure totalled 75,000 to 81,000 men. Of these, 57,000 to 61,000 were combat troops with 41,000 to 42,000 rifles and more than 1,000 light and heavy machine-guns. The force was divided into five corps. [. . .]

Every combat soldier carried one or two hand grenades, every rifle had 70 to 100 cartridges, every light machine-gun was accompanied by 300 to 400 rounds of ammunition and every heavy machine-gun by 500 to 600.

All units . . . had an ample supply of radios, field telephones, and other means of communication. This was also true of the two evacuation columns. . . . The first of these, the strategic or command column, included members of the Central Committee. . . .

Support services were the province of the second column. This included a field hospital and various other institutions, as well as groups of Party and Government officials. . . .

Rations, mainly rice and salt, were carried on the person of each participant for about two weeks. After that, we were obliged to tap local food sources through purchase or requisition.

The above data demonstrate that it was certainly not a 'nation emigrating' as Edgar Snow purported in *Red Star Over China*. Nor was it a 'precipitate, panic-stricken flight', as Mao Tse-tung later alleged. It was a well thought out operation, painstakingly prepared over time, and, although it did take on the character of a retreat later on, it was not initially regarded as such.

I therefore consider false the standard historiographical version, created by Mao Tse-tung, which claims that the breakthrough of the blockade was the result of military defeat and pressure from the enemy. It was not a defeated army, but a fully intact army, that forced its way through the blockade. Its leaders reached their decision voluntarily, based on the sober reflection that the general strategic situation was worsening. The problem was simple: should an area which was being slowly strangled, which was exhausting its resources, and which offered its armed forces less and less freedom of movement continue to be defended? Or should the active strength of the army be preserved and the necessary latitude secured to wage a mobile war in which the enemy might be defeated and a new soviet base created without giving up the old one altogether?

14) *An estimate of round-worm infestation*
(G.F. Winfield, *China: The Land and the People*, pp. 127–9)
There is another worm parasite found in many parts of the world which is common in China and which clearly illustrates other aspects of the problem of fecal-borne diseases. It is the common intestinal round worm, *Ascaris lumbricoides*. The specific name of this worm, *lumbricoides*, means 'earthworm like.' It is an apt description, for the adult female ascarid is almost a foot long and almost as thick as a lead pencil. The male is two or more inches shorter and about half as thick. [...]
... We found ... that about 95 per cent of all rural people in Shantung province harbored ascarids, and that the average for the entire population was fourteen worms per person. City dwellers in Shantung were 35 per cent positive, with an average of five worms apiece....

On the basis of these figures, if the conservative assumption is made that each of the 400 million rural people harbors twenty worms, and each of the 100 million city people harbors six worms, we may then arrive at an estimate of 8 billion ascarids now living in the intestines of the people of China. If all these worms were strung together they would form a worm 1,221,000 miles long – long enough to wrap around the equator almost fifty times. In total they would weigh 130,900 tons, or equal in weight about two million adult Chinese. Since about half the worms are females, and since each female produces about 200,000 eggs each day, it may be estimated that there are 860 trillion ascarid eggs being passed into the Chinese environment each day – 1,720,000 eggs for every man, woman, and child in China.

Why are these worms present in such astronomical numbers and with such universality among all groups? The principal answer is that the household environment is so universally polluted by children that most of the population is in more or less constant contact with soil in which infective ascarid eggs can be found.

15) *The good earth*
(Pearl Buck, *The Good Earth*, pp. 33–4)
The sun beat down upon them, for it was early summer, and her face was soon dripping with her sweat. Wang Lung had his coat off and his

back bare, but she worked with her thin garment covering her shoulders and it grew wet and clung to her like skin. Moving together in a perfect rhythm, without a word, hour after hour, he fell into a union with her which took the pain from his labor. He had no articulate thought of anything; there was only this perfect sympathy of movement, of turning this earth of theirs over and over to the sun, this earth which formed their home and fed their bodies and made their gods. The earth lay rich and dark, and fell apart lightly under the points of their hoes. Sometimes they turned up a bit of brick, a splinter of wood. It was nothing. Some time, in some age, bodies of men and women had been buried there, houses had stood there, had fallen, and gone back into the earth. So would also their house, some time, return into the earth, their bodies also. Each had his turn at this earth. They worked on, moving together – together – producing the fruit of this earth – speechless in their movement together.

When the sun had set he straightened his back slowly and looked at the woman. Her face was wet and streaked with the earth. She was as brown as the very soil itself. Her wet, dark garments clung to her square body. She smoothed a last furrow slowly. Then in her usual plain way she said, straight out, her voice flat and more than usually plain in the silent evening air, 'I am with child.'

16) *Romantic love*
(Olga Lang, *Chinese Family and Society*, pp. 120–1)
'Madame Wu! Tomorrow morning I am leaving Shanghai. I am going to the front. This time I probably shall not return. I see you for the last time. Here is something I want to give you.' ... Staff officer Lei reached in his pocket, brought out an old ragged copy of *Sorrows of Young Werther* and offered it to Mrs. Wu. Between the pages was a withered white rose. [...]

Werther read by a Chinese officer! This book was written when Europe was undergoing great changes and capitalism was emerging. The European youth of that time passionately identified themselves with the hero of Goethe's novel, adopted his individualism and romanticism ...

Romantic love and individualism, almost unknown in old China, have taken possession of modern Chinese youth. Thousands of young men and women have been deeply moved by Werther's fate and also by the unhappy love of their own romantic hero whose confession has just been quoted. Thousands have read other romances, foreign and Chinese, and are enthusiastic over romantic moving pictures.

Romantic fiction reflects realities. The old rigid separation of the sexes is gone. At college young men and women frequently play games and spend their leisure time together, read the same books, go to meetings and demonstrations together. Young lovers have become almost as common in the parks and streets of Peiping and Shanghai as in New York. There is a difference, however – lovers in China can be seen holding hands, but there is no kissing in public places – the young still observe the old rules of reticence.

Romantic feelings are not confined to the upper classes. A riksha coolie in Peiping may tell you of his love for a neighbor's daughter or of his decision never to marry again after the death of his beloved. A girl in a factory in Shanghai may meet a young man there who may ask her to marry him. And in Wusih girls and boys sing: 'My sister is sixteen, the matchmaker begins to visit us. Keep away, matchmaker, boys and girls marry for love!'

Romantic love does not necessarily mean platonic relations. Among the patients at the Peiping Hospital, whose records I studied, unmarried mothers were increasingly frequent – working-class and middle-class girls. Yet – and this has not been true in the past – many of these pregnancies had had romantic preliminaries.

17) *Lu Hsün's fiftieth birthday party*
(Agnes Smedley, *Battle Hymn of China*, pp. 60–2)
One hot afternoon in the middle of 1930, two teachers, man and wife, called on me and made two requests: one, to contribute articles on India and money to a new magazine . . . ; the other, to rent a small foreign restaurant where a reception and dinner could be given to celebrate the fiftieth birthday of Lu Hsün. Lu Hsün was the great writer whom some Chinese called the 'Gorky of China', but who, to my mind, was really its Voltaire.

The first request I granted readily, but the second was fraught with danger, because the hundred men and women who were to be invited represented the world of 'dangerous thoughts'. My friends assured me, however, that all guests would be invited by word of mouth only and sworn to silence, and that 'sentries' would be posted at street intersections leading to the restaurant. [. . .]

Lu Hsün, accompanied by his wife and small son, arrived early, and I met, for the first time, the man who became one of the most influential factors in my life during all my years in China. He was short and frail, and wore a cream-coloured silk gown and soft Chinese shoes. He was bare-headed and his close-cropped hair stood up like a brush. In structure his face was like that of an average Chinese, yet it remains in my memory as the most eloquent face I have ever seen. A kind of living intelligence and awareness streamed from it. He spoke no English, but considerable German, and in that language we conversed. His manner, his speech, and his every gesture radiated the indefinable harmony and charm of a perfectly integrated personality. I suddenly felt as awkward and ungracious as a clod. [. . .]

It was a motley and exciting gathering – pioneers in an intellectual revolution. One group, poorly dressed and apparently half-starved, was pointed out as representing a new modern aesthetic theatre trying to edge in social dramas between Wilde's *Salome* and *Lady Windermere's Fan*. A more prosperous-looking group proved to be Futan University students led by Professor Hung Sheng. They had produced some of Ibsen's plays. . . . A third dramatic group was made up of young Leftist actors, writers, and translators who had produced plays by Romain Rolland, Upton Sinclair, Gorky, and Remarque. . . .

From my place at the gate I now saw a number of people approaching. One tall, thin young man walked rapidly and kept glancing behind him; he was clearly a student, and as he passed, my friends whispered that he was the editor of the *Shanghai Pao*, underground Communist paper which conducted a kind of journalistic guerrilla warfare in the city. Shortly after came one whose foreign suit was wrinkled and whose hair was wild and dishevelled. He had just come from months in prison. . . . [. . .]

After the dinner, speeches began. . . . When the man with the wild hair made a report on prison conditions, we watched every move of the servants. After him came the editor of the *Shanghai Pao*, giving the first factual report I had so far heard on the rise of the Red Army and on the 'harvest uprisings' of peasants who had fought the landlords and then poured into the Red Army like rivulets into an ever-broadening river.

A short, heavy-set young woman with bobbed hair began to tell of the need for developing proletarian literature. She ended her address by appealing to Lu Hsün to become the protector and 'master' of the new League of Left Writers and League of Left Artists, the initial groups which later became the Chinese Cultural Federation.

Throughout, Lu Hsün listened carefully, promptly turning his attention to new speakers, his forefinger all the while tracing the edge of his teacup. When all had finished, he rose and began to talk quietly, telling a story of the half-century of intellectual turmoil which had been his life – the story of China uprooted. [. . .]

He was now asked, he said, to lead a movement of proletarian literature, and some of his young friends were urging him to become a proletarian writer. It would be childish to pretend that he was a proletarian writer. His roots were in the village, in peasant and scholarly life. Nor did he believe that Chinese intellectual youth, with no experience of the life, hopes, and sufferings of workers and peasants, could – as yet – produce proletarian literature. Creative writing must spring from experience, not theory.

18) *Child labour in China*
(R.H. Tawney, *Land and Labour in China*, pp. 149–50)
. . . If conclusions may be drawn from the inquiries hitherto carried out, it would seem reasonable to say that, with the exception of certain individual establishments, which have pursued a more intelligent policy, the conditions generally obtaining in factory employment recall those of the first, and worst, phase of the Industrial Revolution in England. Not only are hours preposterously long, and wages almost incredibly low, but part of the work is often done by relays of cheap or unpaid juvenile workers, sometimes imported from the country, and occasionally, it is alleged, actually sold to their employers, in shops which are frequently little better than barns, and in which the most elementary conditions of health and safety appear to be ignored. It is possible, in certain cities, to go through a succession of these little establishments, which may or may not be technically factories, largely staffed with boys between eight and sixteen years of age, working twelve to fourteen hours per day for seven days in the week, and sleeping at night on the floor of the shop, in which the lighting is such as to make it certain that the sight of many of them will be permanently

injured, machinery is completely unguarded, the air is loaded with poisonous dust, which there is no ventilation to remove, and the buildings are unprovided, in spite of municipal by-laws, with emergency exits, with the result that, in the event of fire, some proportion of the workers will almost certainly be burned.

19) *The New Life Movement*
(R.V. Hemenway, *A Memoir of Revolutionary China*, pp. 168–9)
After Christmas 1936, I became interested in the New Life Movement, which the Nationalist government now sponsored. . . . This movement had been launched to promote the old Confucian standards of *I* (regulated attitudes), *Li* (right conduct), *Lien* (honesty), and *Ch'ih* (integrity). The basic idea behind the movement was to reform the Chinese people, to build a sound economy and to sponsor the rebirth of the Chinese nation.

Dr. Huang and Miss Liu took me to my first New Life Movement meeting. This was a woman's meeting. It was held in a big auditorium and policed by chubby young girls in police uniforms who zealously evicted squalling babies and their mothers from the audience. . . . The meeting's general theme was that everyone should do work with her hands. The speaker told us that it was an old-fashioned idea that it was undignified for those with money or position to work. She went on to say that it was wrong for any student to be exempted from work. She argued that study was indeed necessary but that it should not go unbalanced with manual labor. In my opinion, if this idea could be accepted by Chinese intellectuals, it would be another big step forward in the formation of a new China. The room displayed a fine exhibit of handwork, mostly sewing and embroidery, which was designed to impress the visitors to go home and also learn to make such things.

On the way home I asked more about this new movement. Dr. Huang and Miss Liu told me that, among other things, the goals were clean living, elimination of extravagance, elimination of squeeze and graft, and the prohibition of smoking and spitting in public. The movement aimed to raise the standard of living of the Chinese and create a new society. The leaders of the movement hoped to prepare the Chinese people to move from an agricultural way of life to that of an industrialized state. The New Life Movement was thus conceived of as one element in China's effort to modernize. . . .

One immediate effect of the movement could already be seen in the more courteous conduct of the police, conductors, and other public servants.

'Trains go on schedule now,' one remarked proudly.

'And they are clean,' added another.

'Smoking and spitting are not allowed now anywhere on Nanchang streets.'

'No one can go around with buttons unbuttoned.'

The new ethic also applied to foreigners. One of the men missionaries in Nanchang was politely approached by a policeman who asked him to button all the buttons on his overcoat.

20) *Students at Peking National University*

(Harold Acton, *Memoirs of an Aesthete*, p. 340)

The sop to Cerberus was a course on modern English poetry, and this time there could be no doubt that the students were satisfied. The lecture-room was always packed, and many took notes which were amplified in the literary reviews. The professors of English at other universities smiled sarcastically when they heard I was lecturing on T.S. Eliot. But I felt justified. China's new generation was in revolt against deadening rhetoric, irrelevant descriptions of nature, and ossified poetical diction. European science had also undermined, if not destroyed, its absolute beliefs.

The grey disillusionment of *The Waste Land* was natural to it. The obscurities of that poem were due to the eclecticism of Eliot's method, and even this had a precedent in Chinese poetry, which bristles with symbols, interpolations, and allusions historical and mythical, and frequently has lines from other poems incorporated in the text. These difficulties acted as stimulants rather than deterrents. Several students took the trouble to wade through Miss Jessie L. Weston's *From Ritual to Romance*, and one wrote a thesis on the poetry of T.S. Eliot. Yeats and de la Mare had a few votaries but aroused less general interest: perhaps they were not contemporary enough for my contemporary-famished students. All had read *Lady Chatterley's Lover*, of which a cheap pirated edition was available in the Tung An Market, hence Lawrence's poems had a certain *succès de scandale*.

21) *Wanton destruction in Peking*
(L.C. Arlington and W. Lewisohn, *In Search of Old Peking*, foreword)
What would one naturally wish to see first in Peking? This book, it is
hoped, will tell you, not only what to 'See First,' but 'WHAT TO SEE'
worth the telling from A to Z. But, as it is about 'Old Peking,' it
describes not only buildings that are to be seen to-day, but also those
that have disappeared completely.

Readers may be led to believe that the authors have sometimes
mixed up the two, when during their rambles round Peking they are
unable to find monuments or buildings that are mentioned in the book
as still existing. This, unfortunately, is not the fault of the authors . . .
but is due to the indifference of the Chinese themselves, more
especially of their authorities, towards the historical monuments in
which Peking is so rich. . . .

One might, perhaps, pass over minor acts of vandalism, such as
converting historic palaces into modern restaurants and tea-houses;
famous temples into barracks and police-stations; cutting down
ancient cypresses to sell for firewood; defacing age-old walls and
tablets with political slogans, and so forth. But in many instances
historical buildings and monuments have actually been destroyed by
official orders. The work of destruction culminated in 1933 with the
removal of the entire priceless collection of Palace Treasures to the
South, where they are stored in the vaults of banks, the beautiful
paintings doomed to be eaten by moths, or destroyed by the damp.
[. . .]

That the Chinese people, formerly so attached to their own culture
and customs, should have acquiesced in this wanton destruction . . . is
not only surprising, but is of serious ill-omen for the artistic and
cultural future of the country as a whole. This is not written in a
carping spirit or the narrow view of a foreigner: many Chinese think
the same, and say so quite freely.

22) *The hard-won honors of longevity*
(George N. Kates, *The Years that were Fat*, pp. 95–6)
I have seen old gentlemen riding silently in glass-paned coaches, a
footman leaping down from behind to guide the horses round a corner,
who were living examples of what seventy or eighty years of the
old-fashioned discipline finally could do, in China, to the human

frame. They might be bowed with the years, shrunken even, but majesty dwelt consciously upon their white heads. They invariably wore such colors as darkest green, the browns and grays of tree bark, or dull steel, or else a quite indefinable purple-blue-black; relieving the simple cut of their gowns usually with a single idiosyncratic touch, as for example in summer a fan made of eagle's feathers, with perhaps a crystal pendant swinging from its spotted bamboo handle, or a spectacle case of green sharkskin or of black satin embroidered with metal thread.

I have never seen old age more grandly self-respecting, or more self-justifying. The modern Westerner loses enormously by not comprehending what high ranges, both of appearance and conduct, are accessible to those who have actually cultivated their later years. This single mistake, and the consequent mismanagement of all our possibilities from middle age onward, puts us worlds apart from those Chinese within the traditional system. We wax happily, but wane with ineptitude. The last part of life we tend to abandon even to despair, whereas for the Chinese it is a summit, for the very reason that it has been built by human wisdom alone upon a notoriously fragile and transitory base.

These hard-won honors of longevity could not be assumed too lightly by anyone without severe censure. My servants would quickly comment if a man only in his forties began to cultivate his beard. 'It is not fitting for So-and-So,' they would say, 'to stop being clean-shaven, and to affect drooping whiskers, when the time for these has not yet arrived!'

23) *Newspaper readership in China*
(Carl Crow, *Four Hundred Million Customers*, pp. 170–2)
Partly for the benefit of our clients, and partly in order to satisfy a natural curiosity on such statistical matters, we have gone to a good deal of trouble to arrive at a reasonable conjecture as to the number of newspaper readers there are in China. Since there is no audited circulation, figures and the claims made by publishers reflect future hopes rather than past performances. . . . [W]e have a fair idea as to the circulation of the leading papers (less than a hundred) with which we do business. The statistics of the Chinese customs show how many tons of newsprint are imported into the country each year. Since the

domestic production of newsprint is so small as to be negligible, it is rather an easy matter to figure out the maximum number of average-sized newspapers it would be possible to produce from this newsprint supply. Then we have accurate figures as to the number of newspapers and other periodicals that are transmitted through the Chinese Post Office. . . . We also have fairly complete information as to the press equipment of the papers, know which ones cannot possibly print more than 2,000 copies daily. . . . We carry a lot of advertising containing coupons which people can send in to us with a few cents in stamps and receive in return samples of tooth paste, pen nibs, toilet soap or lipsticks. . . . We figure that if an advertisement in a newspaper with a known circulation of 10,000 pulls 100 coupons and the same advertisement in another newspaper of unknown circulation pulls 50 coupons, we are fairly safe in setting down the circulation of the latter paper at 5,000. From these four sources of information . . . we arrive at the conclusion that the total number of purchasers of daily newspapers in China is approximately 3,000,000. This includes innumerable small 'mosquito' papers which earn a precarious livelihood by blackmail. . . .

The figure of a circulation of 3,000,000 daily newspapers indicates that less than 1% of the population of the country are newspaper readers, but that figure presents an inaccurate picture. Every important newspaper enjoys what we call a 'secondary' circulation. Many newsboys in Shanghai sell their papers on what might be properly called a rental basis. . . .

. . . No one can make more than a blind guess as to how much this secondary circulation amounts to. It may triple or possibly quadruple the total of 3,000,000 daily papers printed, but with the most optimistic guess, the fact remains that the total number of daily newspaper readers in China is a good deal less than 5% of the total population. That may represent a very gloomy picture, but there is a brighter side to it. . . . [I]t is more than twice as large as it was fifteen years ago.

THE SINO-JAPANESE
WAR AND THE
CIVIL WAR

The task of reporting fully on the Sino-Japanese War, which broke out in earnest in 1937, was beyond the ability of the handful of western journalists who remained in China. Theodore White and Annalee Jacoby admitted frankly that much of what was written was based on press conferences and communiqués, and added, 'We used phrases the world understood to describe a war that was incomprehensible to the West.'[1]

However, on occasions, western journalists and observers did happen to be in the right place at the right time: James Bertram, a free-lance writer from New Zealand, reached Sian in December 1936, shortly after the mutiny and kidnapping which led to Chiang Kai-shek reversing his policy towards Japanese encroachment on China (1). Rhodes Farmer, of the *Melbourne Herald*, was an eyewitness at the battle for Shanghai from October to November 1937 (2). It was testimony from westerners who remained in Nanking when the city fell to the Japanese in December 1937, and who reported the atrocities committed by the victors, which strengthened world opinion against Japanese aggression and presented the Chinese people in a more sympathetic light than at any time since the eighteenth century (3). Two epic events occasioned by the Japanese invasion were recorded by westerners: Frank Oliver witnessed the deliberate breaching of the dikes of the Yellow River in June 1938 (4), and Hubert Freyn described the dramatic relocation of some of China's universities (5). W.H. Auden and Christopher Isherwood, having been commissioned to write a travel book about the East, chose to go to China and to write about the Bad Earth, the term they used to describe the scourge of war (6). John Gunther brashly revised the stereotypes of the Chinese and Japanese, to the advantage of the former (7).

At first, this admiration was directed uncritically at all aspects of Chinese resistance. But when a split appeared between the Communists and Nationalists, western attitudes to the two sides began to polarize. A new and attractive image of Chinese Communism surfaced, disseminated by those few westerners who reached the Communist wartime capital at Yenan. The Communists were presented (or presented themselves) not only as valuable allies against the Japanese, but also as energetic and moral reformers, in contrast to the corrupt Nationalist regime at Chungking. The first and most famous report was Edgar Snow's *Red Star over China*, based on a visit to Yenan in 1937 (8). Edgar Snow's wife, Nym Wales, spent many hours recording the life histories of Communists (9). Other visitors who confirmed Snow's enthusiastic description included James Bertram, who recalled a theatrical performance, given at the headquarters of the 359th Brigade of the Eighth Route Army in north Shansi, which illustrated the propaganda message used by the Communists (10). Violet Cressy-Marcks, who reached Yenan in 1938, was impressed by the role of women in that same force (11). The army itself was the subject of a careful analysis by Evans F. Carlson, until recently of the United States Marine Corps (12). Theodore White and Annalee Jacoby described the Chinese Communist leadership (13). Claire and William Band – the latter had been a university lecturer in Peking – were impressed by the Communists' attempt to encourage science in the Border Regions (14). The most influential description of the later Yenan period was by John S. Service, an American career diplomat who accompanied the United States Army Observer Mission – called the Dixie Mission because it went into 'rebel territory' – which reached Yenan in July 1944. The mission portrayed life under Chinese Communism as the mirror-image of life in Chungking under the Nationalists. For this it was subsequently accused of having played a part in the 'loss' of China to Communism (15). For Harrison Forman, the term 'Communism' was no longer applicable to a group of reformers who had ceased to take their lead from Soviet Russia (16).

The contrast lay with the situation in the part of China controlled by the Kuomintang. Graham Peck painted a tragic picture of the methods of conscription employed there (17). Leland Stowe, a journalist with the *Chicago Daily News*, made frustrated efforts to expose the racketeering on the Burma Road (18). Theodore White defied the attempt by the Chungking government to conceal the extent of the Honan famine of 1943, and traced it to official incompetence (19). General Joseph W. Stilwell, 'Vinegar Joe', commander of the United States forces in China, used his diaries to express his fury towards Chiang Kai-shek ('the Peanut') for his failure to co-operate in the campaign to retake Burma. In September 1944 he recorded in verse the moment when he gave Chiang a telegram containing a sharp demand for action on the part of the Chinese government. It was a short-lived victory: a month later Stilwell was recalled and the United States' commitment to Chiang was reaffirmed (20).

After the Pacific war was over, a few writers, for example Father Carlo Suigo, drew attention to the Communist threat (21). But criticisms of the Nationalists continued and multiplied after the outbreak of civil war, when revelations appeared about the use of censorship and the failure to control inflation (22). In contrast, the journalist Jack Belden wrote a classic description of the Civil War from the Communists' perspective, noting in particular how they gained the support of the peasants (23). A. Doak Barnett, a Fellow of the Institute of Current World Affairs, was in China for two years from the autumn of 1947. He visited most of the areas held by the Nationalist government and spent six months in the area controlled by the Communists. His general conclusion was that by 1949 the collapse of the old order was so complete that the Communists moved into a power-vacuum. This collapse even affected Shanghai, the most important bastion of support for the Kuomintang (24). Some western observers, although disenchanted with the Kuomintang government, anticipated that a Communist victory would terminate their role in China, and their comments became increasingly pessimistic. Lt Colonel Robert B. Rigg castigated the 'pillbox psychology' of the Nationalist troops in Manchuria (25). Henri Cartier-Bresson, in words as well as in photographs, described the dying moments of the Nationalist government (26).

1) *Mutiny at Sian*
(James M. Bertram, *Crisis in China*, pp. 150–5)
What part did the Communists play in the Sian affair? Contrary to general belief, they had nothing at all to do with the capture of Chiang Kai-shek. There was certainly a good working understanding between the Reds in the North-west and Chang Hsueh-liang. But the initiative in the events of December 12th came from the Young Marshal and his group of Tungpei 'radicals.' There were no Communists present at the night meeting which planned the coup; the Chinese Soviet headquarters at Pao An, in north Shensi, knew nothing of the plan until they heard, with unconcealed rejoicings, of the arrest of the Generalissimo. Naturally enough it was a situation that they were eager to turn to their own advantage. And they did not have to wait long for an opportunity.

Immediately after the mutiny, the Young Marshal sent a plane to the North to bring representatives of the Soviet Government to Sian. They were invited to take part officially in the negotiations and organisation in the 'rebel' capital, where a new authority was formed in what was called the Military Council of the United Anti-Japanese Armies of the North-west. The small Communist delegation which arrived in Sian, unaccompanied by any Red Army forces, was – as it proved – to exert an influence which effectively determined the whole course of the movement in the North-west. It included Po Ku – bespectacled, owlish, slow-spoken – a former Secretary of the Communist Party and one of its best theoreticians; Chou En-lai, Yeh Chien-ying, and a few others. Of them all, Chou En-lai, the Political Commissar and former assistant to Chiang Kai-shek, was to play the most prominent part in the weeks that followed.

2) *Chinese resistance in Shanghai*
(Rhodes Farmer, *Shanghai Harvest*, pp. 81, 84)
In Chapei the sacrifice to defence had caused even more havoc than Japan's tons of high explosives.

No wonder the Japanese Army was months behind its boasts. Every street was a defence line and every house a pocket fort. Thousands of holes had been knocked through walls, linking the labyrinth of lanes into a vast system of defence in depth. Every intersection had been made into a miniature fortress of steel and concrete. Even the stubs of bomb-battered walls had been slotted at ground level for machine-guns and rifles. This would have to be taken yard by yard by infantrymen: Japan's aggregation of artillery and bombers was not sufficient to reduce this great area. [. . .]

On the way back we were again caught flatfooted, this time by a real bomber. There was no cover. We were in a mud hut area beside Soochow Creek. There and then I learned how the Chinese dodge bombs. I shadowed a Chinese officer. He quickly noted which way the wind was blowing. Then he stood upright, stealthily moving counter clockwise to the planes circling directly overhead. Not for a second did his eyes leave the belly of the aircraft. Four black objects came tumbling out. That was the signal. He raced about sixty yards into the wind and then jumped into a hole. I landed on top of him. The place where we had been standing was blown to bits.

As we hurried along the road leading back to the Settlement we passed a number of soldiers down on their haunches beside Soochow Creek washing blood and muck from their bodies. They had been sleeping in a building a few yards from the bombing. Here was China's resistance in a nutshell: these young stoics who had just missed death a few seconds earlier could still grin up at the urgent departure of the foreign excursionists into their battle area.

3) *A foreign resident's description of the rape of Nanking*
(H.J. Timperley, *What War Means*, pp. 20–2)

Nanking, China.
X'mas Eve, 1937.

What I am about to relate is anything but a pleasant story: in fact it is so very unpleasant that I cannot recommend anyone without a strong stomach to read it. . . .

It is now X'mas Eve. I shall start with say December 10th. In these two short weeks we here in Nanking have been through a siege; the Chinese army has left, defeated, and the Japanese has come in. On that day Nanking was still the beautiful city we were so proud of, with law and order still prevailing: today it is a city laid waste, ravaged, completely looted, much of it burned. Complete anarchy has reigned for ten days – it has been a hell on earth. Not that my life has been in serious danger at any time; though turning lust-mad, sometimes drunken soldiers out of houses where they were raping the women, is not, altogether a safe occupation; nor does one feel perhaps, too sure of himself when he finds a bayonet at his chest or a revolver at his head and knows it is handled by someone who heartily wishes him out of the way. For the Japanese Army is anything but pleased at our being here after having advised all foreigners to get out. They wanted no observers. But to have to stand by while even the very poor are having their last possession taken from them. . . while thousands of disarmed soldiers who had sought sanctuary with you together with many hundreds of innocent civilians are taken out before your eyes to be shot or used for bayonet practice and you have to listen to the sound of the guns that are killing them; while a thousand women kneel before you crying hysterically, begging you to save them from the beasts who are preying on them; to stand by and do nothing while your flag is taken down and insulted, not once but a dozen times, and your own home is being looted; and then to watch the city you have come to love and the institution to which you had planned to devote your best deliberately and systematically burned by fire, – this is a hell I had never before envisaged.

We keep asking ourselves 'How long can this last?' Day by day we are assured by the officials that things will be better *soon*, that 'we will do our best', – but each day has been worse than the day before. And now we are told that a new division of 20,000 men is arriving. Will they have to have their toll of flesh and loot, of murder and rape? There will be little left to rob, for the city has been well-nigh stripped clean. For the past week the soldiers have been busy loading their trucks with what they wanted from the stores and then setting fire to the buildings. And then there is the harrowing realization that we have only enough rice and flour for the 200,000 refugees for another three weeks and coal for ten days. Do you wonder that one awakes in the night in a cold sweat of fear, and sleep for the rest of the night is gone? . . .

Every day we call at the Japanese Embassy and present our protests, our appeals, our lists of authenticated reports of violence and crime. We are met with suave Japanese courtesy, but actually the officials there are powerless. The victorious army must have its rewards – and those rewards are to plunder, murder, rape, at will, to commit acts of unbelievable brutality and savagery on the very people they have come to protect and befriend, as they have so loudly proclaimed to the world. In all modern history surely there is no page that will stand so black as that of the rape of Nanking.

4) *A river changes course*
(Frank Oliver, *Special Undeclared War*, pp. 208–10)
At this point the Chinese army acted with speed and decision which seemed very un-Chinese and which is generally believed to have been the result of the insistence of foreign military advisers. Excavations had been made in the banks of the Yellow River so that they could be quickly destroyed and an enormous stream of flood water sent roaring across country in the path of the advancing Japanese.

... Troops guarded these cuts and at a given signal the cutting continued until water began to trickle through. Natural forces did the rest. Within a matter of hours wide gaps had been cut by the river and a stream of flood water was pouring across the Honan plains between Chengchow and Kaifeng.

It took the Japanese army completely by surprise and soon mechanized equipment had to be abandoned in mud and water. The town of Chungmow was soon surrounded by the silt-laden flood and the Japanese troops advancing on Chengchow took refuge within the town walls, the gates being closed and sandbagged to keep out the flood. [. . .]

The Japanese army and press were loud in their denunciations of this manoeuvre, one of the most effective by the Chinese during the whole course of the war. The Japanese press painted a tearful picture of the sufferings of the unhappy Chinese peasants and claimed that 300,000 had lost their lives in the flood. . . . The figures of Chinese loss of life were grossly exaggerated. The loss of life must have been comparatively small. The exact figures may never be known.

In the first place the majority of the peasants in that area had already left their land and gone south or west. The amazing movement of population from the war areas has been a marked feature of this war. In addition the peasants near the Yellow River knew that for at least a month the banks had been partly cut ready for flooding. . . . [. . .]

Less than a week after the break in the river banks I flew over the floods in a Japanese military plane. The small breaches had by then joined up and three-quarters of the flow of this mighty river was pouring through a gap 400 yards wide. The river had, in effect, changed its course from east to south-east. . . .

5) *Universities on the march*
(Hubert Freyn, *Chinese Education in the War*, pp. 46–7, 49–50)
The record perhaps, as far as number of stop-over places is concerned, was established by the National Chekiang University, originally located at Hangchow. The following description of its wanderings is taken from an article, written by one of the University's faculty members. . . .[2]

'It was a march in a double direction. Backward step by step from the Japanese advance and forward toward a new Chinese national ideal. [. . .]

Our destination was a little town called Kienteh, about a hundred miles up the river. A few of us went by car, bus, or bicycle, but the majority of students and professors went upriver on small, crowded river steam-boats and later on junks. We could, of course, take only a part of our personal belongings, but the university managed to save most of the working material such as the chemistry and physics laboratories, all the foreign books in the university library, and the most valuable third of the Chinese books. Only the machines of the faculty of engineering had to be given up.

After we left Hangchow, we lived and worked always under the most primitive conditions, thus proving that a university does not depend on buildings and comfort but simply on the spirit of teachers and students and a minimum equipment.

The university remained in Kienteh until the end of December. Temples and ancestor halls were made into lecture rooms and dormitories. Wooden partitions, benches, tables, and a blackboard were all that was needed. The requirements for dormitories were equally simple: wooden berths and a *p'ukai*, the Chinese bedding, which everybody carries with him, tables and chairs or stools. It was a lovely little place, which soon became crowded with students. But we could not stay long because of the Japanese advance.

From the beginning it had been the idea of the university not to move to such places as Hankow, Chungking, or Changsha, where most of the other Chinese universities of the war regions had been concentrated and partly amalgamated. If the Japanese advance was forcing the universities to move, it was as well to make the best of the situation, to correct the old mistake of concentration, to go to districts which never had much contact with academic life, and thus to combine university education with the development of the Chinese "interior".'

6) *A visit to the war front*
(W.H. Auden and C. Isherwood, *Journey to a War*, pp. 106–8)
From the top of the pass the view opened. We were looking down the slopes to Li Kwo Yi, with the Grand Canal beyond, . . . not a shot to be heard, not a puff of smoke to be seen – the meadows still and peaceful in the afternoon sun, the blossom beginning on the hill-sides and, in the distance, a blue range of mountains. Auden made me laugh by saying thoughtfully: 'I suppose if we were over there we'd be dead.'

From here we looked down on War as a bird might – seeing only a kind of sinister agriculture or anti-agriculture. Immediately below us peasants were digging in the fertile, productive plain. Further on there would be more peasants, in uniform, also digging – the unproductive, sterile trench. Beyond them, to the north, still more peasants; and, once again, the fertile fields. This is how war must seem to the neutral, unjudging bird – merely the Bad Earth, the tiny, dead patch in the immense flowering field of luxuriant China. [. . .]

On the bridge, just outside Li Kwo Yi, sentries stopped us and examined our passes and cards. We were told that we must first see General Chang Tschen, whose headquarters are at Ma Yuan, a village about two miles to the east. . . . The sun was just beginning to sink, and Ma Yuan, in the distance, with its walls and rookeries and square, church-like towers, looked so lovely that we could almost cheat ourselves into believing that this wouldn't, on closer inspection, prove to be just another huddle of mud and bamboo huts. From a mile away it couldn't have appeared more beautiful and august if it had housed the combined culture of Oxford, Cambridge, and the Sorbonne.

And indeed, despite the soldiers, the horses, the hens, and their symphony of smells, there was something very academic, dignified and gentle about the bespectacled officers who received us. General Chang Tschen himself is mild and stout, in carpet slippers. His first words were an apology for the quality of the supper we were about to eat. . . .

'So you wish to visit the front? Ah. . . .' The officers looked puzzled and mildly discouraged. 'The front line is very dangerous.' 'Yes, we have heard that.' 'Ah. . . .' There was a pause of polite deadlock. We felt very apologetic for our own obstinancy. Then the telephone rang and the General answered it, in accents which, to our western ears, have always the ring of resigned, dignified despair: 'Wa? Wa? Ah. . . . Ah. . . . Ah. . . .' 'We are told', he informed us, 'that the Japanese will soon begin to shoot with their gun. Please do not be alarmed. It is only a very small gun. . . .'

7) *Men in armour and men in undershirts*
(John Gunther, *Inside Asia*, pp. 43–4)

The Japanese are more stubborn than the Chinese, and less logical. The Chinese are infinitely less efficient than the Japanese, and more disillusioned. In China your visiting card is more important than your passport; in Japan your passport is considerably more important than your visiting card. The Japanese possess those virtues which a cynic might consider rather dull, industriousness and an exaggerated tendency to hygiene, for instance. The Chinese on the other hand have all the charming vices. They love to flirt, to waste time in amiable conversation, to meditate, to gamble. The Japanese never smoke opium. But they make money selling it to the Chinese. The Japanese are men in armour, carrying a machine-gun; the Chinese are men in undershirts, wondering when it is going to rain. If you ask a Japanese to choose between spending the rest of his life on an island with either a Chinese or an Englishman, he will pick the Chinese who would presumably become his slave; the Chinese, confronted with a similar choice, would almost certainly pick the Englishman, who he assumes might be educated to become his equal. The Japanese are fanatics. The Chinese are almost indescribably reasonable.

8) *Soviet strong man*
(Edgar Snow, *Red Star Over China*, pp. 79–80, 83–4, 87)

I met Mao soon after my arrival: a gaunt, rather Lincolnesque figure, above average height for a Chinese, somewhat stooped, with a head of thick black hair grown very long, and with large, searching eyes, a high-bridged nose and prominent cheek-bones. My fleeting impression was of an intellectual face of great shrewdness, but I had no opportunity to verify this for several days. Next time I saw him, Mao was walking hatless along the street at dusk, talking with two young peasants, and gesticulating earnestly. I did not recognize him until he was pointed out to me – moving along unconcernedly with the rest of the strollers, despite the $250,000 which Nanking had hung over his head. [. . .]

Mao seemed to me a very interesting and complex man. He had the simplicity and naturalness of the Chinese peasant, with a lively sense of humour and a love of rustic laughter. His laughter was even active on the subject of himself and the shortcomings of the Soviets – a boyish sort of laughter which never in the least shook his inner faith in his purpose. He is plain-speaking and plain-living, and some people might think him rather coarse and vulgar. Yet he combines curious qualities of *naïveté* with the most incisive wit and worldly sophistication.

I think my first impression – dominantly one of native shrewdness – was probably correct. And yet Mao is an accomplished scholar of Classical Chinese, an omnivorous reader, a deep student of philosophy and history, a good speaker, a man with an unusual memory and extraordinary powers of concentration, an able writer, careless in his personal habits and appearance but astonishingly meticulous about details of duty, a man of tireless energy, and a military and political strategist of considerable genius.

The Reds were putting up some new buildings in Pao An, but accommodations were very primitive while I was there. Mao lived with his wife in a two-roomed *yao-fang* with bare, poor, map-covered walls. He had known much worse, and as the son of a 'rich' peasant in Hunan he had also known better. The chief luxury they boasted was a mosquito net. Otherwise Mao lived very much like the rank and file of the Red Army. After ten years of leadership of the Reds, after hundreds of confiscations of property of landlords, officials and tax-collectors, he owned only his blankets, and a few personal belongings, including two cotton uniforms. Although he is a Red Army commander as well as chairman, he wore on his coat collar only the two Red bars that are the insignia of the ordinary Red soldier. [. . .]

Mao impressed me as a man of considerable depth of feeling. I remember that his eyes moistened once or twice when speaking of dead comrades, or recalling incidents in his youth, during the rice riots and famines of Hunan, when some starving peasants were beheaded in his province for demanding food from the yamen. . . .

Yet I doubt very much if he would ever command great respect from the intellectual *élite* of China, perhaps not entirely because he has an extraordinary mind, but because he has the personal habits of a peasant. The Chinese disciples of Pareto might think him uncouth. I remember, when talking with Mao one day, seeing him absent-mindedly turn down the belt of his trousers and search for some guests

– but then it is just possible that Pareto might do a little searching himself if he lived in similar circumstances.

9) *Hsiao K'ê, youngest general*
(Nym Wales, *Red Dust*, p. 131)
In 1932, when he was only twenty-three years old, Hsiao K'ê was given command of the noted Sixth Red Army, and became the youngest of the top commanders of the Chinese Communist army. His name soon became very well known in China. After he had joined his forces with those of Ho Lung in the Hunan-Hupeh soviet area, these two men at the head of their flying columns made history move fast.

In this perpetually mobile army, Hsiao K'ê was without doubt the most mobile single unit. During my interview with him, he was constantly making short maneuvers, sliding along benches, striding about the room, pounding the table, and, on any provocation, bursting forth with lyrical slogans. He had had thirteen wounds, however, and was entitled to a certain amount of nervousness. [. . .]

I found this boy prodigy refreshing to talk with because he was bristling with exact facts and figures – unlike most Chinese, who take very little interest in mathematical details. Hsiao K'ê was in himself a complete revolution against the old Chinese humility of manner. He knew his worth and was not shy of appraising it. It was characteristic of him that he had kept a diary of all the one hundred seventy battles he had engaged in, and when I asked how many times he had been wounded, he wrote down the exact dates on a slip of paper. He did everything to a finish and never stopped at the Confucian halfway point. Like Chou Ên-lai, Hsü Hsiang-ch'ien, and Mao Tsê-tung, Hsiao K'ê is a revival of what the Chinese call the 'military scholar'.

10) *Theatrical propaganda among the partisans*
(James Bertram, *Unconquered*, pp. 274–5)
That afternoon, we were invited to an outdoor performance by the Drama Group. For three hours or so, we sat in the open, in the beginning of a snowstorm, to watch the show.

The chilly weather did not deter this massed audience of soldiers and peasants. We all squatted on the ground before the open stage that is to be found in the center of most Chinese towns and larger villages, and that is normally used for official meetings and by old-style traveling companies. In the 'wings', a large wood fire had been provided for the performers, for after all they had the worst of it.

As usual, the star turns were given by the children, and their dancing – which, under these conditions, certainly deserved it – earned hearty roars of approval. I was interested to see that the choice of plays had been carefully suited to this country audience; it was a definitely 'lowbrow' performance. The Japanese officer who figured so frequently always had his face painted white like the conventional Chinese villain; all the pieces were short, full of action, and intelligible even to the fur-capped village children who swarmed around the front of the stage, or perched precariously in the bare branches of neighbouring trees. It was first-class entertainment, and no political point was allowed to be lost.

The finale – and again, this was characteristic – was a 'Beggars' Dance' to an old Chinese folk-song that is universally known: *Lien Hwa Lou*, 'The Falling of the Lotus'. It has a catchy tune that you may hear sung anywhere in the streets of North China. . . .

. . . In a free English rendering, with repetitions, it runs something like this:

We are all poor friends together, without food to eat,
Poor friends, picking one flower blossoming, a single lotus flower!
We walk together along the road, the road of hunger and cold,
Walk together, two flowers blossoming; the flower opens and the lotus falls.

But new words had been found for the old song, and the audience was not slow to take them up.

Those who want to fight the invaders, set your hands to work! the leader would sing. And the chorus was deafening:

All the Japanese robbers together cannot stop our iron fist! An hour later, everyone in the town was singing the song, to the new words.

11) *Red Amazons*
(Violet Cressy-Marcks, *Journey into China*, pp. 184–6)

I was anxious to find out what part women played in this strange army, and one crispy morning I went out of the North Gate and started to climb to reach the school for wives of men fighting in the anti-Japanese war. I was shown over the dormitories. They were the same kind of cave dwellings that I have described before, but here on the *k'ang* there was room for nine persons, with the wall at the back of their heads, and made in the rock an alcove on which were placed chopsticks, toothbrush, soap and mug, sometimes a few books and a mirror; a towel hanging on a nail usually completed the sum total of their belongings. . . . Some of the women had cut out flowers and trees from books and stuck them on the walls. Nearly all had a clean piece of paper tacked up behind their towel. Rules were pasted up neatly upon a white piece of paper, which sometimes was bordered by a coloured piece, but I never saw a chair, table or any piece of furniture in these caves. They showed me their copy-books. I learned that, though the women of the Eighth Route Army had sometimes military training and all were drilled, yet they never went into battle, though they were often used for dangerous messages; their chief work was political, organising, propaganda, teaching, nursing and being librarians.

I asked where they all were. . . . They said they were below the mountain, lined up waiting for me to come down and watch their drill and address them.

I felt a bit nervous, and even more so when, lined up in four long, straight rows, I found women standing at attention in the Eighth Route Army uniform. They all looked terrifically strong and healthy, and the female sergeant gave them orders. They drilled really well. I was told they had been waiting anxiously ever since I had arrived at Yenan for me to address them. I had to, of course. After it was over, I was asked, would I answer questions. I agreed. Too late I found out I should have had beforehand a political economy course. . . . I did my very best, but I was quite warm in the icy air, though standing still, and was glad when the order came to charge the mountain. They raced ferociously towards it, getting up somehow from the point charged, though there were no paths, and I thought it would be impossible. Up they went to the top. . . .

Outside some of the caves ... about twenty women assembled. They took up positions. The hefty sergeant stood on one side playing a tune for them on a mouth organ and the cultural class commenced. The dance was truly well done, but seemed more suited for budding ballerinas than the practical, rather stout red-faced women in breeches and uniforms. I would never have believed that these women could poise, balance and be so graceful.

Gone were the resolute-looking eyes and sticking-out jaw. Thus encouraged, I asked if they always slept in caves and never saw their husbands, and they said some of their husbands were in Yenan and once a week they stayed out at night. . . . I asked if they had babies. They replied they did, and asked if I would like to see them. I said I would, and so followed them around the cliff corner, climbed a little higher and entered a cave where the *k'ang* went the whole length of the cave; lying on it at 2-ft. intervals were about twenty babies. It was feeding-time, and all were sucking contentedly at their bottles. There was no improvisation here. The bottles were good, and so were the teats. I asked about the milk and was surprised to find it an expensive brand of American tinned dried food. They were sweet babes and were being very well looked after; all were clean. I asked the Principal if she thought the mothers of these babies were learning at the school things which would help the country more than if they each cared for their own baby, and if the baby would make as good a man or woman. She said, of course, because looking after a baby did not require a woman's whole individual attention, and it would make no difference to it growing up with a good or bad character.

12) *The Eighth Route Army*
(E.C. Carlson, *The Chinese Army*, pp. 35–7)

The Eighth Route Army is the military instrument of the Chinese Communist Party. It has discarded the idea which prevails in Occidental armies that a leader, in order to be effective, must be accorded privileges and be set on a pedestal. Leadership is based entirely on merit. Even the customary labels by which military categories are known in Western armies have been discarded. The group which is customarily known as 'officers' is called 'leaders'. The balance of the men of the army are known as 'fighters'. . . .

Both leaders and fighters are indoctrinated with the qualities of honesty, humility, selflessness and truthfulness. There is created in each individual the desire to do what is right. It is right to perform the duties which are assigned by competent authority. Therefore, the desire to perform one's duty becomes almost an obsession.

. . . When a subordinate approaches a leader of higher rank (authority) the manner of the former is formal and he salutes according to the custom which obtains in Western armies. But – when the subordinate is off duty he is on a basis of equality with the leader, and the two may sit down and chat together. . . . The material condition of the leader is the same as is that of the fighter. The quality of the clothes, food and sleeping accomodations does not differ.

In order that the rank and file of the army may attain political knowledge and a high ethical standard, the system of political commissars is employed. . . . Training periods for the troops are divided in the ratio of sixty percent military instruction to forty percent political indoctrination. . . . The illiterate are taught to read and write. They unite in the singing of patriotic songs. Each company has a club in which opportunities are provided individuals to express themselves.

The rules and regulations for the government of the army are as follows, although here again persuasion is the guiding principle:

Major Rules
(1) Execute the anti-Japanese patriotic principles.
(2) Execute the instructions of higher leaders.
(3) Do not take the smallest thing from the people.

Minor Rules
(1) Ask permission before entering a house. Before leaving thank the occupants for their courtesy, and ask them if they are satisfied with the condition of the house.
(2) Keep the house clean.
(3) Speak kindly to the people.
(4) Pay for everything that you use, at the market price.
(5) Return all borrowed articles.
(6) Pay for all articles which the army has broken or destroyed.
(7) Do not commit a nuisance (dig latrines).
(8) Do not kill or rob the captives.
[. . .]

Another potent force in creating universal good will and tolerance is the emphasis which is placed on the unimportance of material things. The pay of the army ranges from one Chinese dollar per month for the fighter to five dollars per month for Chu Teh, the Commander-in-Chief. Thus, Chu Teh's monthly stipend is less than the pay of a private in the Kuomintang armies.

13) *The Chinese Communist leaders*
(T.H. White and A. Jacoby, *Thunder out of China*, pp. 227–9)

The leaders of the Chinese Communist Party were a highly interesting group. They could be studied only from the outside, for what went on in their inner councils was a tight secret. Their primary characteristic was their sense of unity. They had been fighting together for twenty years, against the Kuomintang and then against the Japanese; their families had been tortured, murdered, lost. . . .

The leaders had the character of an elite. They were cocky, some of them arrogant. No such burden of politics and administration as plagued the harassed officials of Chungking weighed them down. Conversations with them were pleasantly unhurried sessions; they reflected on policy for meditative hours, and when interviewed, they might talk on and on about any particular point of theory that struck them as important. They were above the tangle of paper work; they thought for the long range, while trusted juniors executed their decisions. These leaders lived with little of the ostentation of Chungking's topmost officials, though they had cleaner homes and better food than the rank and file. They made no fetish of equalitarianism. Here was no such vast gulf as separated a Chungking cabinet minister from his shivering, threadbare office clerk; but physical distinctions of comfort and convenience were accepted as needing no comment or justification.

Though the leaders were recognized and accepted as the elite, they prided themselves on their democracy, and they hewed out for themselves a code of manners to match their professions. Party policy had decreed a production drive after the Kuomintang blockade in 1941 to make the Yenan area self-sufficient. Peasants had been urged to expand their sowing and harvesting. All government officials and party members were expected to cultivate land in order to raise their own food and lift the burden of their support from the local peasants. This drive had been superlatively successful, and the party and its functionaries lived not on taxes but on the sweat of their own brow. Mao Tse-tung tended a tobacco patch; before the war he had smoked cheap Chinese cigarettes, but now, to keep himself in smokes, he toiled at his tobacco plants and raised enough for all party headquarters. Chu Teh, the commander in chief, grew cabbages. Most of the senior leaders prided themselves on their approachability. Mao, it is true, lived in a suburb several miles beyond the town and was exalted above ordinary mortals. But the others dealt casually with all comers. At the regular Saturday evening dances at Communist army headquarters, where music was supplied by a sad collection of horns, paper-covered combs, and native string instruments, Chu Teh sedately waltzed about with little office girls, and the burly chief of staff, Yeh Chien-ying, gayly accepted invitations to two-step from any maiden who had enough pluck to ask him.

These simple, earthy men did not look like any terrible threat to Chungking and world stability. But when you examined their thinking and listened to their conversation, you found a stubborn, irreducible realism. The first thing you noticed was their knowledge of China. They knew their own country thoroughly and understood the villages. They were engineers of social relationships, and they knew precisely what the peasants' grievances were and precisely how those grievances could be transmuted into action. . . .

Their ignorance of the outside world was sometimes shocking. They knew little of high finance, protocol, or Western administration; their understanding of industry, Western engineering, and international commerce was primitive. They knew Western history only as interpreted by Marxist classics. . . . But they knew down to the last detail the impact of the Western world on China and how they planned to harness the energy and technology of the West for the benefit of the peasant.

14) *Guerilla Science Congress, Hopei Border Region, 1942*
(Claire and William Band, *Dragon Fangs*, pp. 151–3)
The conferences were held at the Border Government village. About a hundred scientists were present, and this created considerable strain on the facilities of the village. . . . It was at the height of the fly season and the heat was terrific.

The chief food was plain rice gruel, served piping hot; bean curd soup was almost the only other hot item. These were paraded through the village street, supposedly covered from the flies. In the dining-room we kept everything covered the whole meal through. Anyone anxious for something to eat would sing out:

'All get ready!' A wave of the hand over the table and 'Bzzzzzz. . .' go the flies. Someone lifts a cover, we all take a hasty chopstickful, and down drops the lid before the flies can get inside. [. . .]

The conference room was a newly repaired schoolroom that had been wrecked the previous autumn by the Japanese. Long new planks resting on clay brick pillars served both as benches and desks for the conference members. We noticed that although these planks were freshly cut only a few days prior to the meetings, their white surfaces were already spotted all over with fly-mark. The bowls of hot drinking water that were served out from time to time to quench our scientific thirst, were at once accepted by the flies as convenient parking places during the discussions; average count, twenty per bowl.

At the conference, the Association was in fact founded with five branches: agriculture, medicine, radio, engineering, and teaching; all intensely practical in outlook. Yet at the first open meeting Bill [Band] was asked to read a paper on the properties of liquid helium at minus 271° C., and there was a keen discussion after it, too. But the main business of the conference was a discussion of a number of reports on the practical work done to date in the region by the scientific and technical workers employed by the Border Government. Iron-smelting, reports on the work we had seen the previous February; cast-iron factories; oil-cracking; leather-tanning; medical work; grain storage; extension work among the peasants by the Bureau of Agriculture. There was also an exhibition arranged by the Bureau of Agriculture: life histories of local plant diseases and insect pests; samples of improved grain, local handicrafts and the products of home industries; improved goats, sheep, pigs and chickens.

It was an amazing experience. Here we were in the roughest of possible environments, completely surrounded by Japanese and cut off from everywhere, attending a scientific conference. . . .

. . . Here we found Chinese intellectuals with no false pride or intellectual snobbery, with courage enough to face life with the peasants even through the dangers of war-time. We felt proud to find so many of the graduates and students from our modern universities among them. They are planning to return to Peiping after the war, but not to the old ways, the artificial academic life, isolated from the real life of the country. They have learned an unforgettable lesson: their social responsibility for the welfare of the peasant population. . . .

15) *We have come into a different country*
(John S. Service, *Lost Chance in China*, pp. 178–81)

July 28, 1944

Although I have been in Yenan only six days, it seems advisable . . . to try to record a few general first impressions of the Communist Border Region. [. . .]

All our party have had the same feeling – that we have come into a different country and are meeting a different people. . . .

There is an absence of show and formality, both in speech and action. Relations of the officials and people toward us, and of the Chinese among themselves, are open, direct and friendly. Mao Tse-tung and other leaders are universally spoken of with respect (amounting in the case of Mao to a sort of veneration), but these men are approachable and subservience toward them is completely lacking. They mingle freely in groups.

Bodyguards, gendarmes and the claptrap of Chungking officialdom are also completely lacking. To the casual eye there are no police in Yenan. And very few soldiers are seen.

There are also no beggars, nor signs of desperate poverty. [. . .]

Morale is very high. The war seems close and real. There is no defeatism, but rather confidence. There is no war-weariness.

One gets a feeling that everyone has a job. The program to make every person a producer has a real meaning. Those who do not grow crops work at something like spinning. [. . .]

There is a surprising political consciousness. No matter who one questions – barber or farmer or room attendant – he can give a good description of the Communist program for carrying on the war. We notice that most of the coolies waiting on us read the newspaper. [. . .]

We saw a group of men marching down the road with no armed escort in sight. We were told they were new recruits.

16) *'Are they Communists?'*
(Harrison Forman, *Report from Red China*, pp. 176–9)

For Americans, Communism has always been a big bogy. The average American will grudgingly admit that the Russians have done a pretty good job at fighting the Nazis, but he still wants no truck with their Communism. Two questions arise, then, in con-sidering the Chinese Communists: First, what is their connection with Soviet Russia? Second, how Communist *are* these Chinese Communists?

Answering the first question, I can say this: In the five months I spent with the Chinese Communists I saw not the slightest tangible connection with Russia. There were no Russian supplies – no guns, planes, or equipment. There were no Russian military or political advisers. The sole Russians in the Border Region were a surgeon who seemed to stay at the operating table about sixteen hours a day, and two representatives of the Tass News Agency. . . .

Occasionally I saw portraits of Marx and Lenin; but these seemed like relics of a revolutionary past. For every portrait of Marx or Lenin I found a hundred of Roosevelt, Churchill, Stalin, and Chiang Kai-shek. The portraits of these four hung everywhere – in government offices, in shops, in army barracks, in peasants' huts. Stalin's was there not as the leader of Communism but as the head of one of the United Nations. . . .

Here is the answer: the Chinese Communists are not Communists – not according to the Russian definition of the term. They do not, at the present time, either advocate or practice Communism. It is true that in the early days, when the Chinese Communist Party was founded, Marxian Leninism constituted the philosophy and the practical guide of that party. But, as the years moved on, the CCP found it increasingly hard to persuade the individualistic Chinese peasant to exchange his ambition to be master of his own little patch of land for faith in the new-fangled collectivism. Repeated compromises were required, until today the Chinese Communists are no more Communistic than we Americans are. I discussed this point with Mao Tze-tung. . . . [. . .]

'To begin with,' he said to me, 'we are not striving for the social and political Communism of Soviet Russia. Rather, we prefer to think of what we are doing as something that Lincoln fought for in your Civil War: the liberation of slaves. In China today we have many millions of slaves, shackled by feudalism'. . . . [. . .]

'In trying to liberate these millions and improve their livelihood by means of agrarian reforms, however, we do not intend to go so far as the Russian Soviets – to take the land from the landlords and redistribute it to the people'. . . . [. . .]

'Politically, too, we differ from them in that we neither call for nor plan a dictatorship of the proletariat. We do not advocate a collectivism that discourages personal initiative – in fact, we encourage competition and private enterprise'.... [...]

'As for government – as you know – we believe in and practice democracy, with the one-to-three system to limit any possibility of one-party dictatorship as practised by the Kuomintang today. In this respect, too, we differ widely from the Russian Soviet system.... [...]

'But then,' I demanded, 'if you don't practise Communism, why do you call yourselves Communists?'

His reply was that the name was a carry-over from the old days. 'You've seen enough here to confirm what I've been saying,' he added; 'enough to know that we are no longer Communists in the Soviet Russian sense of the word.'

17) *Conscription in Shensi, 1941*
(Graham Peck, *Two Kinds of Time*, pp. 217–18)

Several times that spring, batches of new conscripts were herded through Shuangshihpu, and since they had not the training which gave a soldier's life a minimum value to his masters, they were treated with a more casual brutality. The worst group I saw was about one hundred and fifty men who had already been goaded up several hundred miles of highway from Chengtu and had another hundred or more ahead of them before they reached their 'training camp' in Sian.

I shall never forget the afternoon they were herded into the village. It was splendid sunny weather.... Slowly around a bend in the yellow road staggered the long line of spectres, their flapping black rags thick with dust, their faces gleaming pale as the distant snow. They were roped together of course, and they cruelly jerked and cut each other as they lurched about. Many seemed delirious, staring wildly and talking to themselves. Some inhumanity toward conscripts was usual enough to go unremarked but this was a surpassing case, and there was a startled hush on the busy Shuangshihpu street as their guards drove the groaning, panting, gibbering creatures into the barns which had been requisitioned as their night's lodging.

That evening there was much gossip, interested if not indignant, and the stories of those who had talked to the conscripts or their guards were widely circulated. It was said they were opium smokers, beggars, and other riffraff cleaned off the streets of Chengtu for the New Life Movement. They had been sent on this walking trip with the idea that most of them would die and the rest of them become real conscripts. The villagers who lived near the requisitioned barns reported they were given no bedding. Coming from frostless Chengtu, dressed in thin cotton, many had already become sick during the freezing mountain nights. It was also reported they were fed nothing but a little porridge made chiefly of water. Some said the guards had admitted to underfeeding them by policy, to make them so weak they would not try to escape.

But the conscripts still had one way out. Next morning, before the party was whipped off again, the guards laid out on the riverbank, then thriftily stripped, the frail bony corpses of four starved and exhausted men.

18) *The Burma Road racket*
(Leland Stowe, *They Shall Not Sleep*, pp. 68–9)

In Kunming, while I was there, a new Buick car was delivered over China's war-purpose lifeline and sold for six thousand American dollars to a wealthy Chinese. The owner would buy black-market gasoline, stolen from Chinese government trucks by Burma Road drivers (or officials), for $1.50 a gallon. Along the road there were scores of government-owned Dodge trucks standing idle, rusting in the rain, because no spare parts were available for them. But in private-owned accessory shops in Kunming anyone could purchase parts for Dodge trucks or cars. They had simply been lifted off the stranded trucks down the road, the trucks which should have been busy carrying war materials up into China.

When I asked why some seventy or eighty per cent of the tonnage which came over the Burma Road was gasoline, somebody laughed and said: 'Well, petrol is a splendid commercial commodity, isn't it?' Admittedly one third of every truck's cargo had to be gasoline to be used as fuel for its round-trip journey; and high-octane gas was indispensable for the Chinese air force. But Kunming showed a great number of private cars in circulation. Black-market gasoline could always be found.

19) *The Honan famine*
(T.H. White and A. Jacoby, *Thunder out of China*, pp. 169–70)

Each large town along the way had at least one restaurant open for those whose purses were still full. Once we ordered a meal in such a restaurant, but for us the spicy food was tasteless. Hungry people, standing about the open kitchen, inhaled the smell with shuddering greed; their eyes traced each steaming morsel from bowl to lips and back. When we walked down the street, children followed crying, 'K'o lien, k'o lien (mercy, mercy).' [. . .]

There were corpses on the road. A girl no more than seventeen, slim and pretty, lay on the damp earth, her lips blue with death; her eyes were open, and the rain fell on them. People chipped at bark, pounded it by the roadside for food; vendors sold leaves at a dollar a bundle. A dog digging at a mound was exposing a human body. Ghostlike men were skimming the stagnant pools to eat the green slime of the waters. . . .

When we awoke in the morning, the city was a white sepulcher peopled with gray ghosts. Death ruled Chengchow, for the famine centered there. Before the war it had held 120,000 people; now it had less than 40,000. The city had been bombed, shelled, and occupied by the Japanese, so that it had the half-destroyed air of all battlefront cities. Rubble was stacked along the gutters, and the great buildings, roofless, were open to the sky. Over the rubble and ruins the snow spread a mantle that deadened every sound. . . .

The quick and the dead confused us. Down a side street a man trundled a wheelbarrow with a figure lying passively across it. The inert form was dressed in blue rags, the naked feet covered with goose-pimples; it stirred and quivered and seemed alive, but the bobbing of the head only reflected the roughness of the road.

20) *Chiang Kai-shek receiving a telegram from President Roosevelt* (Joseph W. Stilwell, *The Stilwell Papers*, p. 334)

> I've waited long for vengeance –
> At last I've had my chance.
> I've looked the Peanut in the eye
> And kicked him in the pants.
>
> The old harpoon was ready
> With aim and timing true,
> I sank it to the handle,
> And stung him through and through.

The little bastard shivered,
And lost the power of speech.
His face turned green and quivered
As he struggled not to screech.

For all my weary battles,
For all my hours of woe,
At last I've had my innings
And laid the Peanut low.

I know I've still to suffer,
And run a weary race,
But oh! the blessed pleasure!
I've wrecked the Peanut's face.

21) *The Children's Army*
(Father Carlo Suigo, *In the Land of Mao Tse-tung*, p. 78)

4th August [1945]

Last night there were more discussions among the [People's Soldiers], this time the [Children's Army] taking part. The Communist school-master spoke, reiterating the rules for the protection of the district, and, at the end of every sentence, asking them if they understood. He finished by saying:

'I have spoken to you very clearly about your duty. Anyone who is caught not carrying out orders will be punished. Do you understand?'

They all said 'yes'. The leader of these miserable little creatures got up. If one had heard, without seeing him, this boy of not more than thirteen, one would have said that he was a man very conscious of his power. He allocated his followers to their different posts and emphas-ized again the laws that governed their corps. There was a whistle, a word of command, and all marched off in military formation.

All this astonished us. It seemed unbelievable that this secret and evil power, which manifested itself in deeds of terror, should have succeeded in attaching to itself these young things so that each understood his special task and responsibility, and acted in a way worthy of a better cause.

The district, the roads, the cross-roads, even the paths leading to the mountains, are under the surveillance of these young Communist forces. Anyone who travels, even the mandarin or a more important person, must show a permit, saying where he comes from and if asked, how much money he has on him. Permission to proceed depends on the goodwill of the boys. The least suspicion, an indiscreet remark, an unwise smile, anything that annoys them, will be dearly paid for. Anyone who fails to satisfy them is surrounded by these little curs. It is useless to try to run away, for they clutch a person's legs, jump on his back, and shout for the head of the [People's Soldiers] who must always be ready with some armed men. The unfortunate prisoner is taken to the village and tried by the same boys. The trial is terrifying, such is their arrogance and their natural ignorance and incompetence, and yet they decide whether he shall be condemned or pardoned. At the end of the trial the leader asks: 'What sentence shall we give?' If one says, 'Bury him alive,' the unfortunate man is lost. Such is Communist education.

22) *Prices unlimited*
(Lawrence K. Rosinger, *China's Crisis*, pp. 159–60)
For a long time Chinese censors cut out any discussion of the skyrocketing cost of living in dispatches sent abroad. As a result, even a year after China and the United States had become military allies, few Americans knew how serious Chungking's price situation really was. . . .

Today China's catastrophic inflation is no longer a secret. Chungking officials, some of whom were shocked when Wendell Willkie referred to the price situation, hoarding, and profiteering at a press conference during his visit there in October 1942, later began to talk openly about the fantastic cost of living, and even gave figures. Newspapermen were permitted to refer to the extreme shortage of supplies from abroad as a cause of inflation, but even now they may not do more than hint at internal economic conditions, such as hoarding and profiteering, that lie behind a good part of the phenomenal price increases.

Perhaps the degree of inflation China is experiencing can be indicated most vividly by an incident. In the summer of 1943 a one-story, temporary, mud-and-bamboo structure was erected in Chungking alongside a modern three-story broadcasting studio made of brick and stone. Despite the differences between the two buildings their construction costs were the same! The reason? The studio had been put up in 1939 when prices had not yet begun to ascend at an alarming rate. . . .

Today matters are much worse. Children play with dollar bills as they would with paper dolls, and well-to-do businessmen go about accompanied by coolies carrying bulging satchels filled with paper currency. A few figures will tell the story. If wholesale prices in Free China during the war years are compared with wholesale prices prevailing during the first six months of 1937, the following table of approximate price levels can be drawn up:

June 1938 – 1¼ times as high as January–June 1937
June 1939 – twice as high
June 1940 – 5 times as high
June 1941 – 13 times as high
June 1942 – 40 times as high
June 1943 – 140 times as high
June 1944 – over 500 times as high

Who bears the burden of inflation? Everyone agrees that China's students, teachers, intellectuals, government servants, private office workers, army officers, soldiers, and others with comparatively fixed incomes have suffered disastrously from soaring prices. This is so not only in the capital, but throughout Free China.

23) *Teaching the clods of the soil*
(Jack Belden, *China Shakes the World*, pp. 167–8)
Illiterate, suspicious, somewhat afraid of the outside world, the peasant was interested not in ideas, not in humanity, not in civilization, but only in himself, his own mud-walled little world.

How teach this ignorant human beast of burden anything? How teach him, for example, those terribly complex Chinese characters that the scholars and the wealthy had monopolized for centuries. . . . How drive into the head of a manure-stinking, ghost-believing peasant a bunch of Chinese characters that he did not want to learn and that hitherto he had got along without? [. . .]

The Communist solution was both simple and typical. They combined education with life. Instead of drilling the peasant in school (except in winter), the Communists began teaching him how to read by showing him characters connected with his daily life and occupation. Thus a shepherd would be taught the characters for sheep, dog, stick, grass and so on. A farmer would learn the characters for field, millet, wheat, mule and the like. The methods of teaching were also as ingenious as they were pleasant. A school child would go around at the noon recess to the homes of five or six housewives and paste on the front door, the living-room table, and the kitchen stove the characters for each of those objects. While continuing to do her work, the housewife would memorize the characters. The next day the schoolboy would bring three new characters. Or, as I saw, a farmer ploughing in his field would put up one character on a big board at each end of the field. Thus, going back and forth all day, even his primitive mind could grasp the complex convolutions.

24) *Riding high for a fall*
(A.D. Barnett, *China on the Eve of Communist Takeover*, pp. 17–20)

Shanghai
November, 1947

[. . .]
Descriptive adjectives alone can hardly convey a true impression of how crowded and hectic Shanghai is today. . . . Between 4 and 5 million people are now crowded into roughly the same area in which 3 million lived, worked, and played just a few years ago. . . . [. . .]

In terms of real income and consumption, the average standard of living of Shanghai's masses appears to be higher than ever before. This does not mean that everyone is well off, nor does it mean that the city has eliminated poverty. . . . The existence of this relative prosperity is mystifying, in many respects. The mystery might be summarized as follows:

1) Shanghai's trade is hampered and disrupted by runaway inflation, lack of foreign exchange, official corruption and inefficiency, restrictive government policies, and civil war in the hinterland.

2) Its industry, recovering from occupation and war, is hampered by these same factors.

3) The city has a greatly increased population.

4) Yet, the general level of prosperity and the standard of living appear to be higher than in the past.

How? It is difficult to obtain a completely satisfactory answer to this question, but many clues can be found if one examines the present situation closely.

First of all, Shanghai's current balance of trade shows a large surplus of imports over exports, made possible by the use of accumulated reserves of foreign exchange.... More than a little UNRRA material, sent to China for relief purposes, has reached Shanghai and gone no farther.... One sees 'relief' goods sold everywhere on the streets. A larger percentage of Shanghai's industrial products is consumed within the city itself than in years past. China's large inland market has been partially cut off, while the local Shanghai market has grown.

The concentration of money, capital, and wealth in Shanghai is greater than ever before. Large sums of money are sent from Manchuria, north China, Hupeh, Anhwei, and elsewhere.... Also, a very large share of the Chinese government's expenditures is made in Shanghai.... In August, deposits in private banks in Shanghai were estimated to be 56 per cent of total national deposits in such banks. The figure is believed to be even higher now.

There has been a drastic redistribution of wealth and income in Shanghai since the end of the war. Part of this has been the 'natural result' of inflation, but government policy has aided in the process. The result: A small upper stratum has accumulated great wealth, the working class has improved its economic position tremendously, and the middle class has been 'virtually wiped out as an economic class.' The key groups that have profited most are cotton-mill owners, stockbrokers, a few corrupt officials and army officers, and some real-estate dealers....

The working class has done well because wages have been set at a high level and pegged to a monthly commodity price index. Many people assert that this has been dictated by fear on the part of the government of disaffection....

As is usually the case during inflation, the salaried groups have suffered most, and the prosperity of the average working man is due, at least partially, to a transfer of wealth from the middle class. A college professor in Shanghai earns about the same amount as a rickshaw coolie does in a good month, and many organizations are embarrassed by the fact that their professional workers are paid at about the same level as their manual laborers. Government employees are terribly underpaid, and a good deal of the existing corruption is attributable to this fact. . . .

Many of the factors underlying the present economic situation in Shanghai are highly artificial, and therefore temporary, and not a few people feel, as one person said to me, that the city may be 'riding high for a fall.'

25) *'Blue Strategy Loses to Red Tactics'*
(Lt Col. Robert B. Rigg, *Red China's Fighting Hordes*, pp. 255–6)
It became one of my tasks when flying low over Manchuria for the truce teams, to identify those towns which were held by the Nationalists and those controlled by the Communists. The battle lines were never continuously drawn and I remember days when I couldn't even locate a fighting front, for there was considerable maneuver in the spring and early summer of 1946. However, the problem of identifying the political color of a town was not usually too difficult. In the field the troops of both sides looked almost alike from an altitude of 400 feet; the Reds, however, would pot-shot at your plane, and they didn't possess much motor transport. In towns, however, you could never judge by the military activity which army was the occupying power. Over both Communist and Nationalist cities waved the red and blue Chinese National flags, but the key to identity was whether or not the predominantly blue Kuomintang flag flew *with* the National flag. Gradually, as 1946 merged with the year to follow, another difference in the two territories became apparent from the air – moats and trenches. These came to signify government-held cities and railway bridges. The pattern began to appear all over China as these giant trenches slowly ringed the cities. Woven about the moats were systems of barbed wire, abatis, and pillboxes. How many new pillboxes were constructed, no one knows, but they numbered in the thousands. Then there was the inheritance of the thousands of Japanese pillboxes – solid structures of thick concrete and narrow embrasures. The Nationalists were not nearly as thorough as the Japanese in the construction of these installations of defense. The Government forces made pillboxes out of brick, and even mud. One of the most ghastly masses of human flesh and splintered bones that I saw in China, was outside the Shantung city of Yenchow, where one of these brick inclosures took a direct hit from a Red artillery piece at 500 yards range.

Not only did all of these fixed defenses give a false sense of security to Government troops, but they also bred an ill-fated 'pillbox psychology' among Nationalist soldiers. The Communists never built them in any significant numbers. They ditched roads, tore up railroad tracks, and blew bridges in their territories; but they seldom sat down in one place to defend anything.

26) *A human accordion*
(*China: Photographed by Henri Cartier-Bresson*, photograph 13)
On Christmas Eve [1948], the gold yuan dropped from 68 to 93 to the dollar. The Kuomintang suspended all sales of gold and silver for the day. The next day the authorities announced that they would distribute 40 grams of gold per person and the Gold Rush was on. Hordes of people queued up before the doors of the banks on the Bund, some waiting for 24 hours to exchange their paper money. As pressure built up, the line looked like a human accordion, squeezed in and out by invisible hands. Given the panic and hysteria, the police acted with leniency. To control and prevent riots, they only splashed cold dirty water from puddles or prodded the people with the rods used to clean their guns. Even as I watched, the gold-hungry crowd grew into such a mass that the police were immobilized, their arms pinned to their sides. I felt hands searching through my pockets. I smiled, and a man smiled back, nodding his head and producing the only thing he had discovered, a bit of pencil. He returned it to me graciously.

NOTES

1. T.H. White and Annalee Jacoby, *Thunder out of China*, New York, 1946, p. 61.
2. Franz Michael, later a distinguished Chinese historian.

CHINA UNDER
COMMUNISM

Even before the 1949 revolution areas under Communist control had experienced radical change. In 1948, David and Isabel Crook studied the process of confiscation and redistribution of land under the Agrarian Law of 1947, in the village of Ten Mile Inn, 275 miles south-west of Peking (1). In Long Bow, a village in Shansi province, William Hinton recorded the next stage in the process of revolutionary land reform: the investigation of the role of the Party. He described how Party members were subjected to the *gate*, that is the purification of cadre ranks (2).

Derk Bodde, an American Fullbright scholar, was in Peking when it fell to the Communists, and he described the reception of the victors (3). Few westerners remained in the People's Republic for long and much of the information on developments in China at this time came from refugees in Hong Kong. An American journalist, Edward Hunter, first used the term 'brainwashing' to translate the colloquialism *hsi nao* (literally, 'wash brain') to describe the experience which some of them had undergone (4). A few westerners remained in China voluntarily, including Dr A.M. Dunlap, an American ear, nose and throat specialist working in Shanghai. He was highly critical of the new regime and wrote his letters to his family in oblique language to evade censorship (5). Others were detained, for example Allyn and Adele Ricketts who were convicted of espionage and who wrote an account of their experience of thought reform and the psychology of group pressure (6).

From 1954, access to China became easier, although restrictions on where visitors might go and to whom they might talk remained comprehensive. George Gale, a journalist working for the *Manchester Guardian*, accompanied a Labour Party delegation on a three-week visit, and concluded that totalitarianism was matched by evidence of material improvements (7). James Cameron represented the *News Chronicle* and travelled over 7,000 miles in China. He was allowed to meet one of the British prisoners of war from Korea who had refused repatriation, and to visit a prison (8).

The French journalist, Robert Guillain, who worked for *Le Monde*, revisited China in 1954-5 for the first time since the revolution. He reported dramatic changes, which he observed were not appreciated by the governments in Paris and Washington because their diplomats were not allowed to enter China. He gave credit to the Chinese government for achieving material successes, but described them as being at the expense of spiritual and intellectual freedom (9). Simone de Beauvoir, who spent six weeks in China in 1955 as a guest of the Chinese government, countered Guillain's pessimistic description of the mood of the Chinese people, 'One must be laboring under a curious delusion to be able to take them for an army of ants'. For her, the Communist programme was 'the only possible way out for China' (10). Alan Winnington also took a more positive line. He travelled among the minority groups of south-west China, visiting the 'Black Bone' Norsu slave-owners, the Wa headhunters and the Jingpaw jungle-dwellers. By 1957 the government had started to eliminate slavery among these people and to integrate them into majority society (11). Another rare field-report was that of W.R. Geddes, who, in 1956, went back to the Chekiang village which twenty years previously had been studied by the famous sociologist Fei Hsiao-tung (12).

Professor Klochko, one of thousands of Russian scientists sent to China to support the first Five-Year Plan, watched the 'Campaign against the Four Evils' – one of the mass campaigns preceding the Great Leap Forward (13). Memories of that dramatic event were recorded by William Hinton when he returned to Long Bow, the village where he had witnessed the first stages of the revolution (14). The surge of refugees into Hong Kong – one calculation was that one and a half million had fled from the mainland in the decade to 1960 – provided an additional source of information on events in China. Suzanne Labin claimed that her book, *The Anthill*, 'presents the evidence of these first-hand witnesses as to the truth about Chinese communism.' (15). The atmosphere of the period after the Great Leap was conveyed by Sven Lindqvist, a Swedish student who lived in

Peking in 1961–2 (16). Westerners were very restricted in what they could see, but the journalist Charles Taylor by chance observed *hsia hsiang*, the transfer to the countryside of educated youth, at Peking station just before the Cultural Revolution (17). Americans could not go to China, but Lisa Hobbs, a reporter on an American newspaper, did manage to get there. Because she was the holder of an Australian passport, she was granted a visa and went on a tour arranged by Luxingshe, the Chinese tourist bureau (18).

Edgar Snow, in an interview with Mao Tse-tung held early in 1965, found him 'reflecting on man's rendezvous with death', and questioning the role that future generations would play (19). That role became apparent when, in 1966, the Cultural Revolution was launched. Joshua Horn, an English surgeon long-resident in China, associated the political developments with the dramatic medical advances which were being achieved, including the first case of reattachment of a severed limb (20). Other westerners were more sceptical. The Dutch diplomat, Douwe Fokkema, compared the Red Guards and the Destroy the Four Olds campaign (old thought, old culture, old customs, old habits), to the iconoclasm which had swept the northern Netherlands four hundred years previously (21). Anthony Grey, a Reuters correspondent, was kept in solitary confinement for over two years in his house in Peking (22). His description of the Red Guards may be contrasted with more sympathetic accounts of their activities given by Neale Hunter, who taught at the Shanghai Foreign Languages Institute (23) and Joan Robinson, Professor of Economics at Cambridge University (24).

1) *'He's a poor peasant'*
(I. and D. Crook, *Mass Movement in a Chinese Village*, pp. 54–5)
The first to rise was Fu Li-yong, a mild old man who achieved a sinister appearance by knotting the peasant's white towel so far down his forehead that only the lower halves of his eyes were visible. He peered out from under the towel and began:

'I had 8.5 *mu* of land the year before last. And in the spring of last year, the peasant union gave me 1.3 *mu*. So now I have 9.4. I haven't got an animal. I have a hoe, a spade, and a mattock, but none of the big tools like a plow or seeder. I have enough seed, but not enough manure to fertilize more than 3 or 4 *mu*.

There are three of us in the family, but I'm the only one who counts as a workhand. The yield isn't high enough to see us through, so I have to do short-term labor for others.

I have four sections of housing. . . .

The estimated average yield of my land is over 7 *dan*, but the actual crop last year was only a bit over 3 *dan* of unhusked millet and 1 *dan* of corn. . . .

I wouldn't call myself a poor peasant. You can hardly say I have too little land, for even though it doesn't yield enough to feed the whole family, I can make it up with outside work. My wife can spin and weave, and she and my daughter both make clothes'. . . .

Fu Li-yong paused, then added: 'So I think maybe I ought to be considered a middle peasant.'

'How do you think he ought to be classified?' asked Geng Xi.

The fermentation groups huddled together and began to whisper. At last the spokesman of one group stood up and said, 'We think he's a poor peasant. Although he has plenty of land, its yield is low. And even though he has four sections of housing, they're so small that you can't even turn around inside.'

Another speaker rose: 'We think he's a poor peasant too, because he has to work for others to feed his family. And he has no animal.'

Another said, 'He fanshenned only recently – less than a year ago.'

After a lot of whispering among the women, one of them stood up. 'He's a poor peasant, all right. His wife's half crippled, and his daughter's too young to do much. He's the family's only good workhand.'

A young man rose. 'He wasn't really honest. The conditions he described were those of a poor peasant, weren't they? So why did he classify himself as a middle peasant? He should have said straight out that he was a poor peasant.'

At this, Geng Xi asked Fu Li-yong, 'Suppose you didn't do outside work. Would you have enough to eat?'

'Certainly not,' said Fu.

'Well,' said Geng Xi, 'everybody here seems to think you're a poor peasant. What's your opinion?'

'I haven't any,' Fu replied. Evidently he felt that he really was a poor peasant, but that to say so straight out would have been like asking to have his 'hole filled up'.

'Has anyone got anything to add?' the chairman asked.

'No, nothing more,' came from various parts of the room. 'He's a poor peasant.'

2) *Party purification*
(William Hinton, *Fanshen*, pp. 414–15)
More dramatic than any stage play, the Party consolidation meetings inevitably became the centre of all village activity. All day long the thirty-three delegates stood guard at the *gate*. In the evening they met with their respective sectional groups and reported what had happened. The hundreds of rank-and-file peasants who came to these meetings evaluated each day's events and recommended appropriate action in regard to those Communists who had been heard. Then they went on to make accusations and register complaints against those who would be heard on the morrow.

All the grievances of three tumultuous years came to light. So eager were the peasants to make known their opinions and to hear what happened that dozens continued to gather outside the windows of the meeting hall each day. . . . From a campaign which began by involving only a few activists among the people this Party purification took on the proportions of a truly mass movement. . . .

The Party members also met every evening after a full day at the *gate*. They took up the manner in which each comrade had reviewed his or her past and the reaction of the delegates. In an effort to encourage sincere self-criticism, they went over each person's record point by point and demonstrated that the truth, no matter how terrible or embarrassing, met with better response than evasion. . . .

A campaign as intense, as all-pervading as this could hardly have taken place in any but an agrarian community, restricted to grain culture and therefore burdened with a long slack season. In no other private-enterprise society could a whole village have taken the time out to carry through such prolonged meetings. The results promised to repay the effort many-fold.

The village would never be the same again!

3) *The People's Liberation Army enters Peking*
(Derk Bodde, *Peking Diary*, pp. 103–4)

3 February 1949

[. . .]
Today's big event has been the grand victory parade signalizing the

formal take-over of the city. It unfortunately coincided with the first real dust storm of the winter. . . .

Prominent in the parade were thousands of students and workers from schools and organizations throughout the city. Many of their colored paper banners and Mao Tse-tung portraits were torn to tatters by the wind. Among the students also marched some well-known university professors. Some groups danced to the rhythmic drum-and-gong beat of the *yang-ko* or 'planting song' – a simple traditional peasant dance performed in unison by large groups, which is already becoming enormously popular here as the result of the general Communist emphasis upon folk art. More familiar to me was a band of stilt walkers, cavorting merrily in colorful costumes above the heads of the crowd. Other groups, directed by 'cheer leaders,' chanted, as they marched, the famous 'eight points' of Mao Tse-tung.

Of chief interest was, of course, the Liberation Army itself. I missed the first contingents of infantry and cavalry, as well as part of the motorized units. But in what I did see, lasting about an hour, I counted over 250 heavy motor vehicles of all kinds – tanks, armored cars, truck loads of soldiers, trucks mounted with machine guns, trucks towing heavy artillery. Behind them followed innumerable ambulances, jeeps, and other smaller vehicles. As probably the greatest demonstration of Chinese military might in history, the spectacle was enormously impressive. But what made it especially memorable to Americans was the fact that it was primarily a display of *American* military equipment, virtually all of it captured or obtained by bribe from Kuomintang forces in the short space of two and one half years.

And what about the reactions of the civilian participants and spectators? Granted that some of the former paraded only because they had been told to do so, and that many were schoolchildren too young to realize the full significance of what was happening, the fact remains that the enthusiasm of most was too obvious to have been feigned, and this notwithstanding that many had been exposed to wind and dust for some four hours before I saw them. I have no doubt that not a few on this day felt a keen sense of personal participation in an event symbolizing the beginning of a new era in Chinese history. The reaction of the spectators, on the other hand, was, like that of most

Chinese crowds, less outspoken. Nevertheless they seemed in general quite favorably disposed and obviously deeply impressed by the display of power. As the stream of trucks continued, I heard several exclaim with wonder: 'Still more! Still more!'

4) *Ahoy! The Brain!*
(Edward Hunter, *Brain-Washing in Red China*, pp. 3–4)
I stared at the young man sitting in front of me. He was thin and nervous, with long, narrow bones. His face was straw-colored, and his hair, naturally, was intensely black. His slanted eyes were deeply set in drawn skin. Evidently in his late twenties, he was very much Chinese, in spite of his new European clothes. [. . .]

. . . He was Chi Sze-chen (phonetically Mr. Gee), a student who had recently graduated from the North China People's Revolutionary University, which is a few miles outside Peiping, and is the biggest and the most important of China's political indoctrination schools. He was telling me what he had gone through. The story concerned something wholly new in China – 'thought reform,' 'self-criticism meetings,' and the process of Communist Party indoctrination in general as practiced in Red China. The plain people of China have coined several revealing colloquialisms for the whole indoctrination process. With their natural facility for succinct, graphic expressions, they have referred to it as 'brain-washing' and 'brain-changing'.

Brain-washing became the principal activity on the Chinese mainland when the Communists took over. Unrevealed tens of thousands of men, women, and children had their brains washed. They ranged from students to instructors and professors, from army officers and municipal officials to reporters and printers, and from criminals to church deacons. There were no exceptions as to profession or creed. Before anyone could be considered trustworthy, he was subjected to brain-washing in order to qualify for a job in the 'new democracy'. Only then did the authorities consider that he could be depended upon, as the official expression is worded, to 'lean to one side' (Soviet Russia's) in all matters, and that he would react with instinctive obedience to every call made upon him by the Communist Party through whatever twists, turns, or leaps policy might take, no matter what the sacrifice.

5) *Our patient is no better*
(A.M. Dunlap, *Behind the Bamboo Curtain*, pp. 77–9)

June 18, 1951

Your letter of June 4 came in last week-end making a fairly quick and uneventful passage. My guess is that the envelope still contained California air. I wonder how free air and 'controlled' air like being mixed? I was not aware of any commotion! [. . .]

Our patient is no better. The symptoms are much the same but I must not elucidate as there may be resentment if too many details are given. One is free to say that the temperature is still very high with not infrequent convulsions. It is too bad we cannot bring in some of the new medications from the West. [. . .]

This is my day for teaching. My big class of 54 is asking that I give them an extra lecture instead of an examination. The last two classes have had similar treatment. I have no desire to read fifty-four papers. Under the present system most of the newly reorganized medical schools have several hundred students in each class, good, bad and indifferent, and all get the same grade in each section. No one fails and examinations are more for the purpose of telling whether or not the instructor is 'producing the goods'. . . . The end result is that all students entering a medical school are graduated, providing their serious thinking is right. *(For 'serious' read 'political'.)*

Later. When I went into my class at the medical school today, one of my students told me that my Chinese colleague, Dr. L.K., had committed suicide last Saturday. This is a great shock and deprives Shanghai of its foremost Chinese otolaryngologist. . . . He studied under me at the Peking Union Medical College. . . . I had hoped to turn my patients over to him should I be allowed to leave. Man's inhumanity to man!

6) *Having one's innermost self brought out*
(A. and A. Rickett, *Prisoners of Liberation*, pp. 261–5)

'There is a question I would like to bring up,' I said confidently. 'It's about my confession, I don't think the one I have just written is quite right. I still did not bring out clearly why I started giving information to the Consulate. Could I rewrite it again?'

The investigating judge stared at me in cold hostility and for a moment I thought he was going to bite the bit off the end of his pipe.

Then, 'Go back to your cell!' came his curt reply. The loathing and disgust in his voice cut deeper than any whiplash. [. . .]

This time there was no need for the others to insist on my making a self-criticism. On the one hand, I was really frightened. Making a false confession was a serious matter. On the other, I was brutally struck by the realization of my own dishonesty. Gone was the former hollow, academic approach to the understanding of my character. The whole sordid rottenness of it was exposed in a flash of revulson and fear.

For a while I wondered if I had any principles at all, and my whole body burned red hot with shame. I expected a fierce tongue lashing from my cell mates, but this time they were surprisingly gentle.

'You should have learned your lesson this time,' said Liao. 'A selfish mind will go to any lengths to fulfil its desires. Now maybe you can see just being an American doesn't lessen your need for reform.' [. . .]

Having one's innermost self brought out and dissected under the glaring light of self-criticism was a shattering experience, but the resulting recognition of myself made me determined to overcome the weaknesses in my character which had been the causes of these former mistakes.

7) *China has found its panacea*
(G.S. Gale *No Flies in China*, pp. 153–5)

. . . I have no doubt whatsoever that in many respects China is a better place to live in now than it was under the Kuomintang. And I have no doubts, either, that most Chinese certainly think so. Very great improvements have been made in the country. . . . What I found offensive in China was to the Chinese a source of pride.

China has taken to Communist dictatorship like a lost man to a signpost, a tramp to bread and cheese, a megalomaniac to Aladdin's lamp. China now knows where it is going; the Chinese are eating better. Whisk! here is China taking its place in the deliberation of the world's great powers round the Geneva conference table. China has found its panacea.

The Government has a very firm hold on the country, and it seemed to me that the country liked it that way. And Communism has as firm a hold on the official class as that class has on the people. The Government is popular. Communism is popular. The Government works, and if that means a dictatorship, so be it. China is used to dictatorships but this one is the people's dictatorship. I met hundreds of Chinese and there are hundreds of millions of Chinese. I do not know what they think about Communism, but I suspect that those who think anything at all about it like it: all of them, that is, except the 1.64 per cent who are deprived of their political rights by edict. . . . [. . .]

China has been cleaned up. There are no flies in China. There are no piles of refuse in the streets of Peking or Shanghai. The air is sweeter and the smell of Chinese sweat is better than the smell of Chinese excrement. The junky closed market in Peking was cleaner than the average London fishmonger's. I have seen more litter, orange peel, crusts of bread with teeth marks in them, blowing scraps of paper, in the Mall after the Queen has passed by on one of her lesser ceremonial occasions than I saw in the whole of China. There are slums, plenty of them, with mud floors, cracked walls, roofs of straggling plaited reeds, but they are alive with children and not with lice. The prostitutes have gone, and I only saw two beggars and both of them in Shanghai.

8) *The stone walls*
(James Cameron, *Mandarin Red*, pp. 96–9)
. . . the prison was, quite simply, a great textile factory. It is true to say that there was a massive wall, and on top of that an electrically-charged wire barrier. . . . [. . .]

There were two thousand convicts in the Prison of the People's Court of Peking. A hundred and thirty of them were women. Two-thirds of the total were classified as 'counter-revolutionaries'. . . . [. . .]

The Governor said: 'There are four stages of re-education. First there is the explanation of their crime. That is not always easy for people whose standards of behaviour are improperly adjusted. Then there is labour education. After all, few of them ever had jobs of any kind. Then there is production technique – merely how to use the machines. Then there is the Current Events class, the classes for correct ideological thinking and the simpler Marxist-Leninist principles. For the illiterates, there is culture. We aim to teach them at least two thousand characters.'

'Do they all respond?' I asked.

'Most of them. . .'

'And if they are obstinate about that?'

'There are, of course, penalties,' said the Governor. 'The most serious punishment here is Social Rebuke. That is to say, the critical attitude taken up towards the offender by the more progressive comrades. . . .'[. . .]

Back in the factory the machines clattered and thumped; some men plunged hanks of yarn into vats filled with scarlet dye, like blood. The expressionless men and women fed the knitting-machines, churning out socks of violent candy-stripe. . . . Nobody spoke.

'We've had no escapes, ever,' said the Governor, 'no physical punishment, and no escapes. Death? Maybe four or five a year. Then, when the prisoner is – re-educated, and freed, the Labour Bureau tries to get him a job outside. As a matter of fact . . . some don't want to leave. . . .

9) *What have they done to them?*
(Robert Guillain, *The Blue Ants*, pp. 96–7, 104–5, 107)
Factories, building sites, hospitals, crèches, working men's clubs and more factories . . . There are a great many of them, it is true. The Chinese effort is amazing and the work of Chinese hands is prodigious. But what about their heads? Had I [left] myself in the hands of my guides, always ready to suggest a new series of visits and information sessions, I should have been entirely saturated with car trips to cotton mills, dams and steel works and I should have brought back with me an accumulation of notes on the Five-Year Plan – its original figures, its present state, the results achieved and its percentages triumphantly exceeded. . . .

Was I never to hear a few men or women talking naturally amongst themselves after their work? Should I be able to gossip one evening at my ease with ordinary Chinese, and by these I do not mean Chinese chosen for me by the Information Section of the Ministry for Foreign Affairs. Did they think aloud; had they any ideas, political ideas, and above all ideas outside politics? To what, today, do they apply their zest for life, their jokes and their sense of humour? [. . .]

What have they done to them? What in God's name have they done to the Chinese to reduce them to this state? This is the cry of the visitor who knew China and the Chinese of yesterday. It is the question that comes to mind almost at once. For the visitor soon makes a few surprising discoveries, of which these are a few examples: one of the great casualties of the new régime is humour; one of the most noteworthy things to disappear is the intelligent Chinese; and today it is almost impossible to find in China a Chinese with any ideas of his own.

I do not go so far as to say that the new Chinese are unhappy. People could easily confound me by citing the glow of collective life and the organised enthusiasm of group manifestations, which visitors who have never known China find so impressive. To me they appear paralysed and this is what surprised me so much. They were tense, I might almost say constipated. These noisy, yelping people were silent. They had become boring whereas in the old days they were amusing and gay. Away from the official parades and gatherings, the Chinese of today are drab and seem to have retired into their shells. [. . .]

In actual fact, no description can do justice to the reality – or even a fragment of the reality: 600,000,000 Chinese all dressed in the same uniform. At first one is taken aback and, since it is a simple and comparatively new garment, the first impression is by no means unpleasant. A blue blouse, commissar-style or, if you prefer it, '*à la Stalin*' with a military collar and buttoned up the front to the neck. Fountain-pen *de rigueur* in the pocket; trousers of the same blue cotton and a floppy cap of the same material. Girls in trousers, for the most part, and dressed exactly like the men, with straight hair or peasant plaits; not a trace of lipstick or make-up. Millions of copies of the same get-up. Naturally one is quickly surfeited, and this surfeit soon turns to an obsession against this terrifying uniformity. [. . .]

An ant-hill, yes, that is what they have become – ants, blue ants. . . .

10) *The emancipation of the individual*
(Simone de Beauvoir, *The Long March*, p. 164)
The anti-Communists simultaneously accuse New China of demolishing the family and of annihilating the individual: both are lying allegations. Everything in the family that admits of free inter-individual relationships is being preserved, nay, strengthened; what has been done away with is the estrangement of the individual person wrought by an oppressive and imperiously sanctified institution. Reactionaries call this a Machiavellian policy and maintain that its unique purpose is to facilitate collectivizing the land. But it seems to me worth noting that, conversely, economic utilitarianism has an immediate humanistic result. Today in China substructure and superstructure so tightly interlock that in certain spheres they are one; the social factor possesses an economic dimension; but productivity depends on the human factor: the march toward socialism implies the emancipation of

the individual, the affirmation of his right to self-determination. Marriage, motherhood have become free. Love is viewed as something 'progressive.' Far and away from being in contradiction, personal aspirations and duty to country jibe: for the commonweal everyone must strive after his own welfare. The road to collectivization is also that by which the woman is acceding to dignity, the youth to freedom. . . .

11) *A terrible happiness*
(Alan Winnington, *The Slaves of the Cool Mountains*, pp. 24–7)
At noon on such a day I met newly freed slaves for the first time. Theirs was a terrible happiness. Such joy is too mixed when men, women and children are happy only to be sitting in the sun, not to be parted from husbands, wives, children, no more to be spreadeagled and flogged, and yet fearful of the future. . . .

. . . In this tiny rural district, several hundred slaves had been released. Newly-built houses of rammed-earth adobe in Bolo village housed 140 of them and those who were not collecting cloth were sitting stitching it, or merely sitting. Old slaves, young slaves, male, female, beautiful, ugly, brutalised and coquettish, clever slaves and congenital idiots, deaf, blind and lame, with work thickened hands and feet that had never known a shoe, they sat, lay, talked, slept, waiting for someone to tell them what to do next. [. . .]

. . . They come from a wide area, as far afield as Szechwan and Li Chiang. Once caught and taken up into the Cool Mountains . . . chances of escape were few. . . . A runaway slave stood a 90 per cent. chance of recapture and the best he could then hope for was that his captor would be dishonest and keep him as his own slave. . . .

Captured children offered little difficulty to their new masters but adults who had been free took badly to slavery and had to be broken in. This was done normally by chaining, flogging and starvation. I saw one device at Bolo calculated to reduce a new slave to cringing servility – an iron ring which slipped over the knee and locked the bent leg so that it could not be moved or straightened. . . . Captured girls or women gave less trouble and the method of anchoring them by getting them pregnant was both simple and effective.

12) *The kitchen god still in his proper place*
(W.R. Geddes, *Peasant Life in Communist China*, p. 48–9)

All the people I questioned said they had abandoned the religious cult of ancestors. Homage to the husband's ancestral shrine did not occur at the weddings studied. Tombs are cared for, but the periodic ceremonies do not appear to be carried out fully. It would be wrong to say that ancestors are not respected, just as it is a foreign slander on the Chinese people to say that children are encouraged to disrespect their parents, but in both cases the respect is expressed generally in secular terms. At least for the children, the important father-figure now is Mao Tse Tung, whose portrait hangs in every classroom and in every living room. [. . .]

In every house which I visited, except one, I found that a representation of the kitchen god was still kept in the proper place above the stove. Even people who had earlier declared that they had completely abandoned the old religious beliefs and practices, admitted, when asked specifically about the kitchen god, that they kept his paper symbol. They all told me that they no longer made offerings to him. This was probably an overstatement. Almost certainly there must have been some ceremony when the old paper inscription was destroyed and replaced by a new one at the end of the year. It would be truer, probably, to say that the kitchen god has lost status, but that he still remains as a vague censor of household activities.

The one exception was especially interesting. It illustrated the important fact that, although the dominant ideology today is atheistic, other beliefs are not proscribed. . . .

In this one household, I enquired, as usual, as to whether the kitchen god was kept. The head of the household said 'Of course not', and tapped a calendar on the wall. It was a printed calendar issued by some church organization. Further enquiry revealed that there were about ten Christian households in Kaihsienkung. . . . [. . .]

Fei mentions two other aspects of the traditional religion which had importance in the village – the worship of the local god, *Luiwan*, and an annual autumn harvest festival for the local gods responsible for the harvest. We need not discuss them, for they are no longer of importance. They were already practically in eclipse when Fei was in the village. The responsibility for the harvest now rests with the Agricultural Producers' Cooperative, but the temples remain and are kept in repair.

13) *The anti-sparrow campaign*
(Mikhail A. Klochko, *Soviet Scientist in China*, pp. 71–3)
The 'Campaign against the Four Evils' began before my arrival in Peking. During my very first days in the city, my eye was caught by large posters with a picture of a woman in military uniform, a solemn and imperious lady pointing sternly at pictures of a rat, a sparrow, a fly, and a gnat – all four of which were crossed out with heavy red slashes, which meant that the government and Party were calling for their extermination. [. . .]

Several days later, on Sunday, April 20, I was awakened in the early morning by a woman's bloodcurdling screams. Rushing to my window, I saw that a young woman was running to and fro on the roof of the building next door, frantically waving a bamboo pole with a large sheet tied to it. Suddenly, the woman stopped shouting, apparently to catch her breath, but a moment later, down below in the street, a drum started beating, and she resumed her frightful screams and the mad waving of her peculiar flag. This went on for several minutes; then the drums stopped and the woman fell silent. I realized that in all the upper storeys of the hotel, white-clad females were waving sheets and towels that were supposed to keep the sparrows from alighting on the building.

This was the opening of the anti-sparrow campaign. During the whole day, it was drums, gun shots, screams, and waving bed-clothes, but at no time did I catch sight of a single sparrow. I cannot say whether the poor birds had sensed the deadly danger and taken off beforehand to some safer ground, or whether there had never been any sparrows in the first place. But the battle went on without abatement until noon, with all the manpower of the hotel mobilized and participating – bellboys, desk managers, interpreters, maids, and all.

The strategy behind this war on the sparrows boiled down to keeping the poor creatures from coming to rest on a roof or tree, thereby forcing them to remain constantly on the wing, for it was claimed that a sparrow kept in the air for more than four hours was bound to drop from exhaustion. . . .

. . . The whole campaign had been initiated in the first place by some bigwig of the Party who had decided that the sparrows were devouring too large a part of the harvests. . . . Soon enough, however, it was realized that although the sparrows did consume grain, they also destroyed many harmful insects. . . . So the sparrows were rehabilitated. Rehabilitation, however, did not return them to life any more than it had the victims of Stalin's bloody purges, and the insects continued to feast on China's crops. Meanwhile, however, we Russians watched the slaughter of the sparrows with disgust, and those whose names were Vorobyov (which means 'sparrow'), or Mukhin ('fly'), or Komarov ('gnat') – very common Russian names – gloomily joked about the mortal danger that threatened them.

14) *Great Leap, Great Fall*
(William Hinton, *Shenfan*, pp. 218–19)

Each production team sent a group out to make iron. Each group took its own grain, its own set of cooking pots and its own system of supply. Each found a suitable camping spot and immediately built a big mud stove. At first the members slept on the ground in the open. . . . Although each unit set up its own kitchen, each kitchen made hot food available to all who came along. . . . No one kept any records. The commune committee guaranteed grain supplies. . . .

At first each village contingent set up a complete production unit. . . . The iron makers made low furnaces, about six feet high, and lined the floor with firebrick. They piled dry wood at the bottom, then a layer of coal, then a layer of ore, coal, ore, coal and ore until the pit was full. Then they lit it from below. There was not enough power equipment to go around so most of them fanned the flames with winnowing baskets. After about three days they could tap the furnace. As soon as iron poured out they notified the Commune Committee to come and check the results. At Shihhui the results weren't always good. The goal was to tap two tons from each heat but usually they got only one and a half. The iron was too low in quality to process directly and had to be sent on to the mill at Changchih Steel to be reworked. . . . [. . .]

From the descriptions of the pace of the work at this time it is hard to see how anyone kept awake. 'As long as I worked at the iron smelting I made no distinction between night and day,' said Wen-te. 'We began working shifts, but soon abandoned that and just worked straight out, two or three days at a time.'

15) *The People's Communes*
(Suzanne Labin, *The Anthill*, p. 100)

THE NEW FACE OF CHINA

Let us close our eyes and remove ourselves in imagination to the Chinese countryside, opening our eyes there to observe the people engaged in this 'great-mass' labour and living through their days as organised for them by the Communist Party. The first thing we shall see is innumerable small huts and hovels standing deserted, many of them already in course of demolition. These were once the humble homes of the former individual peasant families, the dwelling places of the sons of Han. Let us go into one of them. It is empty and there is no sign of life. Its former inhabitants have been removed to a collective dormitory. The rooms are unfurnished now; not a stick is to be seen. All the bits and pieces have been taken away to the Commune barracks. The kitchen is cold, damp and deserted, and the place sounds dull and hollow like an ice grotto. The dishes have gone too, and the saucepans, and the old poker. Even the door-handles have been removed. And all around is complete silence; there are no chickens scratching in the yard, no pigs snorting in the sty. They have all been carried off to the barracks for chickens and the barracks for pigs, beside the barracks for human beings. The loft is bare, and the bundles of firewood that were once there have also been carried off – requisitioned by the community. In one corner there is a small empty shelf askew on its bracket. Was that the little altar once devoted to the spirits of the ancestors? And, of course, there is no sound of children anywhere. They have been taken away to the barracks for children, called crêches; there they will stay until they are eight years old. . . .

16) *After the Great Leap Forward*
(Sven Lindqvist, *China in Crisis*, pp. 101–2)

Several of the people with whom I had daily contact lived, 'in accordance with the demands of their work' – separated from their families. Apart from consultations about their work, people avoided one another; old friends and neighbours kept themselves to themselves. What could they offer if anyone dropped in? Hot water. What could they talk about? The boils under the plaster on their neck, the hunger swellings on their legs, their son of twelve months, unable to sit up. A silent, icy suspicion divided people from each other. I have never experienced more total isolation.

I remember seeing the face of a woman in front of me in the bus. Protruding teeth, bad-tempered mouth. Eyes narrowed in a malicious stare. Black poker-straight hair with a parting curving up like a white scar. For some diseases of the eye they scrape the cornea. This face looked scraped; it was quite without feeling, imagination or compassion. It was merciless.

It was the happiest day of my stay in China when I eventually won the confidence of those fierce eyes and we were able to talk to each other freely. It is not particularly difficult to meet discontented Chinese intellectuals with a bias towards the West. But they themselves do not feel they are Chinese in the proper sense of the word. You have to pierce through the ideological armour of a loyal and genuinely convinced Communist to find a human being who can give reasons and accept arguments, who dares to doubt, who admits the existence of the informer system, the fear and the use of force, and can explain why he still believes in Communism.

17) *Sending down to the countryside*
(Charles Taylor, *Reporter in Red China*, pp. 180–1)
Almost every day through 1965 there were strange scenes in Peking Station. With their few belongings bundled into knapsacks, droves of teen-agers were boarding railway coaches. Waved on their way by their parents who were often wailing in distress, they were heading off for Shensi, Ningsha, and other remote and rugged areas. They were leaving behind their families, their friends, their city habits. . . . These young people were going to settle permanently in the countryside. In 1965 nearly half a million youngsters left the Chinese cities in this way, according to official statements.

Little was voluntary in their exodus. Having failed to win places at university or even senior middle school, they had been 'directed' to their new posts by the Party. No doubt it all made good practical sense, since Peking, Shanghai, Canton, and other major cities are overcrowded, and housing is still a key social problem. There are too few jobs and too few places in the universities for young people, but vast areas in the interior are underpopulated and only sparsely cultivated. By sending millions of young people to these frontier regions, the regime hopes to ease the pressure on the cities, increase the nation's food supplies, and, as a far from incidental bonus, toughen the bodies of the young and temper their political outlook through hard physical labor.

Many accept their assignments gladly, with patriotic fervor and a sense of adventure. But anyone who saw those station farewells can testify that only part of the story is conveyed by magazine pictures of smiling, bright-eyed youths waving proudly from the platforms of the coaches.

18) *I was speechless with anger*
(Lisa Hobbs, *I Saw Red China*, p. 35)

That night, we went to the People's Cultural Park in Canton to see the acrobatics, for which the Chinese are traditionally, and rightly, famous. The open-air theater, with seating for perhaps 2,000 persons, is situated in the 10-acre park in the center of the shopping district. It was packed with middle-aged and older workers. There were many young people, couples with children, but a noticeable absence of young single people. Later, after becoming better acquainted with China's younger generation, I realized they are probably too busy with night classes and political meetings to take much time out for pure entertainment.

There were two empty rows in the front: shortly after the performance started these were filled with some forty buyers from East European countries. No sooner were these seated, than a group of Chinese workers arrived late; seats were promptly set up for them in front of the buyers! I noticed time and time again that, although the Chinese are consistently polite and helpful to foreigners, they are no longer subservient to them: their own needs, at least in such public places as the theater, are answered with equal consideration.

It was during intermission ... I asked ... if we could see a few moments of the modern Peking opera which was playing in a theater across a tree-lined walk.

We stood in the back row in darkness.

There, on the stage, were two soldiers. One, a Chinese, stood with a bayonet-fixed rifle in his hand. At his feet, cringing on his knees, was a captured GI. The GI clasped his hands, trembled so violently his fear was visible to us in the back row. The Chinese soldier spoke, made a threatening thrust: the GI whined for mercy. The audience shook with laughter.

I was speechless with anger.

19) *Going to see God soon*
(Edgar Snow, 'Interview with Mao', *The New Republic*, 27 February 1965, p. 23)

At dinner Mao had mentioned that both his brothers had been killed. His first wife had also been executed during the revolution and their son had been killed during the Korean War. Now he said that it was odd that death had so far passed him by. He had been prepared for it many times but death just did not seem to want him. What could he do? On several occasions it had seemed that he would die. His personal bodyguard was killed while standing right beside him. Once he was splashed all over with the blood of another soldier, but the bomb had not touched him. There had been other narrow escapes.

After a moment of silence Mao said that he had, as I knew, begun life as a primary school teacher. He had then had no thought of fighting wars. Neither had he thought of becoming a Communist. He was more or less a democratic personage such as myself. Later on, he sometimes wondered by what chance combination of reasons he had become interested in founding the Chinese Communist Party. . . .

'Man makes his own history, but he makes it in accordance with his environment,' I quoted. 'You have fundamentally changed the environment in China. Many wonder what the younger generation bred under easier conditions will do. What do you think about it.'

He also could not know, he said. He doubted that anyone could be sure. There were two possibilities. There could be continued development of the revolution toward Communism, the other possibility was that youth would negate the revolution, and give a poor performance: make peace with imperialism, bring the remnants of the Chiang Kai-shek clique back to the mainland, and take a stand beside the small percentage of counter-revolutionaries still in the country. Of course he did not hope for counter-revolution. But future events would be decided by future generations, and in accordance with conditions we could not foresee. From the long-range view, future generations ought to be more knowledgeable than we are. . . . Their judgment would prevail, not ours. The youth of today and those to come after them would assess the work of the revolution in accordance with values of their own. Mao's voice dropped away, and he half closed his eyes. Man's condition on this earth was changing with ever increasing rapidity. A thousand years from now all of them, he said, even Marx, Engels and Lenin, would possibly appear rather ridiculous.

20) *Reattachment of severed limbs*
(Joshua S. Horn, *Away with All Pests*, pp. 118–19)
... For me, the highlight of the congress was a speech made by the young worker, Wang Cung Po, who mounted the rostrum dressed in his blue denims and, without a trace of shyness, told the distinguished guests about his reattached hand. ...

'Here is the hand,' he said as with a dramatic and intensely moving gesture he raised his right arm and clenched and unclenched the fist. 'My right hand has been given back to me by our socialist society. I swear that I will use it till my dying day to safeguard our good new life.'

Some three years later, on a visit to Shanghai, I got in touch with Wang Cung Po. He was working at his original job, had become a skilled inventor, was deeply immersed in the Cultural Revolution and was a leading member of the Rebel Group in his factory. 'You remember,' he said, 'that I swore to safeguard our socialist society. ... That's why I give every minute of my free time to the Cultural Revolution because its purpose is to make sure that China stays red for ever.'

Using plastic tubing, he had made me a model of a prawn of such artistry and perfection of craftsmanship that the function in the reattached hand must have been excellent. His hand was completely normal in colour, temperature, and texture. Movements of the fingers were practically full but wrist movements were slightly limited and careful testing showed that the skin was not quite as sensitive as the skin on the other hand. He uses the hand normally, does gymnastics and is a keen ping-pong player.

21) *Destroy the Four Olds*
(D.W. Fokkema, *Report from Peking*, p. 20)
The iconoclasm that swept the Northern Netherlands in 1566 constitutes a black page in my country's history. A similar judgement must be passed on the Chinese iconoclasm of 1966. The Chinese leaders understood this immediately, but, if they had the power to check it, they refrained from doing so for fear of extinguishing the revolutionary fire that had just been lit. Cultural loss was the price that had to be paid for the revolution. [. . .]

Initially most of the Red Guards were no older than twelve to seventeen or eighteen years of age. Assisted by even younger children, they did not leave even a single house in their search for supposed revisionism. They smashed the gates, or climbed over the walls that give the Chinese houses their typical individual character, and destroyed or seized everything that was the expression of a personal preference: works of art, porcelain, foreign gramophone records, old books, musical instruments, jewellery. 'Bourgeois' furniture was seized. This included linen cupboards and armchairs. Lorries, loaded with these things, drove to and fro through the city. The goods that had been seized were brought to central check-points or to second-hand shops, where they were sold in aid of the Red Guards who indeed needed money. The Red Guards struck or spat upon elderly people, and forced them to charge themselves with crimes they could not have committed. In the centre of Peking one could see groups of pushing and kicking children, who had exposed old people as members of the 'Black Clique' and forced them to carry boards on which the accusations were written.

22) *In the hands of the Red Guards*
(Anthony Grey, *Hostage in Peking*, p. 102)
The shouting and screaming of slogans was supplemented by the noise of other Red Guards rampaging through the house. Pictures were being flung to the floor and smashed. Typewriters, radios and ornaments were hurled around, books were being scattered, curtains and furniture were being daubed with thick black slogans both in Chinese characters and English. Glass was breaking, nails were being hammered in and glue was dripping on me from a portrait of Mao that was being stuck up above the outside door of the house on the glass fanlight.
Then the crowd suddenly quietened. There was some cheering and some applause. I felt the attention directed away from me for a moment as I remained bent double with only the grey step in my field of vision. Then my chief tormentor was roughly urging me to straighten up. I did so and found dangling before my eyes the body of my cat Ming Ming. He was hanging from the balcony or flat roof above my head at the end of a rope linen line. The noose had bitten deeply into his neck and was concealed by the ruff of fur at his throat. His

back legs hung straight down stiffly and there was no sign of movement from him. He was already dead. I felt a great helpless anger at the mindlessness of what was happening.

Cats and dogs were decreed by the Red Guards to be bourgeois-style pets not consistent with the proletarian-pure way of life in China in the early days of the Cultural Revolution and many had been killed and destroyed in attacks on the Red Guards' Chinese victims.

23) *Red Guards at the Shanghai Foreign Languages Institute*
(Neale Hunter, *Shanghai Journal*, pp. 114–16)
The strife in August [1966] had carried over into the Red Guard groups. Two main student organizations had come into being, both of which included in their ranks some teachers and Party members. . . .

The larger of the two main organizations was the Red Guard Regiment. It had responded to the Shanghai Municipal Committee's call to form Red Guard groups and was therefore part of the city-wide First Headquarters, a body loyal to the Party establishment. In our Institute, the members of the Red Guard Regiment tended to be third- and fourth-year students – many of whom were the children of petty-bourgeois Shanghai parents. They had been admitted to the Institute before 1964, when a policy change had raised the proportion of proletarian children.

The smaller group called itself the Field Army. Most of its members were first- and second-year students, and its leaders were the handful of radicals who had been hitting the administration hard during the first stages of the movement. [. . .]

Judging from our Institute's Field Army, the left-wing students were very disappointed at being in a minority, and they spoke and acted larger than life to make up for it. My wife taught second-year English, and 11 of her 15 students were Field Army members. . . . These boys and girls often came to keep us informed during the movement. They were as cheerful as ever during the preliminary small talk, but as soon as the subject of the struggle at the Institute was broached, they would get very serious, even a little bitter, and soon epithets would rain down on the Party authorities. Why was it, they would ask, that, of 200 Party members in the Institute, only 7 or 8 were in any way affiliated with the Field Army? Why was it that only 6 of the 24 representatives on the students' own Provisional Revolutionary Committee were Field Army members? Clearly, they said, the radicals were the victims of a Party Committee conspiracy.

These youngsters were patently sincere in their indignation. They saw themselves as 'Chairman Mao's good children' and believed that their Field Army was the only group in the Institute that was truly responding to the great call to 'carry the Cultural Revolution through to the very end.' They were convinced that time would justify them and that the majority would eventually join them.

My students were equally sincere, but they held different views. They were third-year English students, and all fifteen of them were staunch Red Guard Regiment members. They did not despise the Field Army, but they felt a rather elder-brotherly sadness that the younger students had taken an erroneous course. They too looked forward to the reunification of the student body, but they were quite sure that *they* were the mainstream of the movement.

What the Red Guard Regiment disliked most about the Field Army was its violence. My students were prepared to admit that revisionism did indeed exist in our Institute, but they maintained that the proper way to expose it was to follow the Sixteen Points and 'use peaceful methods, not violence.' The Field Army, they claimed, was essentially violent in language and action, and the behavior of its members showed no respect for the Party. My students felt that the Party – not only in the Institute but throughout the country – deserved credit for its achievements. If revisionists and bureaucrats had usurped important positions, they were to be rooted out, but, as the Central Committee had consistently emphasized, the guilty were only a handful, and there was no reason to suspect all Party members of heinous crimes.

24) *A factory for blind and deaf workers*
(Joan Robinson, *The Cultural Revolution in China*, pp. 136–7)
The Welfare State in the West has something of the condescending atmosphere of charity. The emphasis in China is not on helping the unfortunate, or even on helping them to help themselves, but rather on calling upon them to contribute something to building socialism. . . .

The factory which I visited in November 1967 was started in 1958 with four helpers, four blind workers and four deaf-mutes. They worked by hand with very simple equipment. Now there are 460 workers, of whom 130 are normal. The handicapped workers have succeeded in learning to manage mechanical equipment. The work is ingeniously arranged so that the blind can signal to the deaf by switching on a light when help is needed to repair a machine. . . .

The Cultural Revolution penetrated even here. The workers felt that the Party branch was contaminated with the reactionary line. The management of the factory was undemocratic. The Secretary of the Party branch did not consult with the workers but behaved like an officer giving orders. The blind workers led a rebellion. At first the Party tried to repress them, but they came to the conclusion in the end that their cadres were not really anti-socialist, but had followed the Liu line out of mistaken loyalty. Now a Great Alliance has been formed and work was going ahead in a good spirit.

It was evident that in the problem of making unfortunate people feel that they are not rejected, that they can be of use not only to their own families but the nation, that they are playing a part in a grand movement, the Cultural Revolution is a great help. Every success in learning to overcome a handicap was not only an achievement for the individual, but a vindication of socialism and the Thought of Mao Tse-tung.

THE CULTURAL REVOLUTION TO TIANANMEN SQUARE

In the early 1970s many westerners continued to cite China as a model to be emulated. Maria Macciocchi, an Italian journalist and Communist member of the Italian Chamber of Deputies, commented:

> There are many today who say that Communism with a 'C' can be found here, in the heart of Asia, an all-powerful safeguard against the disillusionments, temporizations, and stagnation of the struggle in the West.[1]

Her description of China was one of lavish praise (1). The Australian journalist Ross Terrill, who had been to China in 1964, returned after the Cultural Revolution and noted the changes in higher education (2). Ruth Sidel, an American sociologist, visited China in 1971 as the guest of the Chinese Medical Association. Her impression of the improved position of women and the care of children had not been overturned when she wrote a new introduction to her book ten years later (3). Jan Myrdal's *Report on a Chinese Village*, describing a village in Shensi through the words of its inhabitants, had been a best seller in 1962. He went back in 1969 and commented enthusiastically on the Cultural Revolution as seen at village level (4). With reference to industry, Charles Bettelheim saw the start of a transformation of the age-old pattern of labour, and thus the beginning a new chapter in the history of the human race (5).

In February 1972 came President Nixon's trip and the 'opening up' of China (6). Many well-known Americans thereupon visited China and recorded their impressions. J.K. Galbraith compared the American extremes of affluence and poverty with egalitarianism in Chinese society (7); Shirley MacLaine, the film actress, led a delegation of American women to China in 1973 and was enraptured by the relationship she observed between women and men there (8).

Some writers rejected this uncritical view. Foremost of them was the Belgian Pierre Ryckmans, writing under the pseudonym Simon Leys. In *The Chairman's New Clothes*, first published in 1971, he exposed the Cultural Revolution as a power struggle. In *Chinese Shadows* (1974) he continued his criticisms of the Maoist regime, and made fun, for example, of the model brigade of Tachai (9). Claudie Broyelle, a French feminist, looked back with embarrassment at her acceptance of the personality cult of Mao at the time of the Cultural Revolution (10).

Other western writers expressed reservations about other aspects of China. Steven Mosher studied a commune in Kwangtung from September 1979 to April 1980 and concluded, controversially, that the claim that peasants were better off since the revolution was a 'political myth' (11). Vaclav Smil was on safer ground when he challenged the view that Chinese industry was environmentally friendly (12). Stephen Endicott went to Szechwan, the province where his grandfather and parents had been missionaries, and studied No. 8 Brigade of Junction People's Commune, now known again as MaGaoqiao village. He admitted that the 'wholesale flight from collectivism' after 1980 had come as a jolt to him (13). Fox Butterfield, the first correspondent of the *New York Times* to be posted to Peking since the Revolution, was struck by the contrast he found between 'official China', 'cardboard cutouts from the *People's Daily*' and the other, real China, where things were done best by 'going through the back door' (14).

In the 1980s mass tourism started and a literature for tourists appeared (15 and 16). Few travel writers conveyed a more convincing picture than did Colin Thubron. His visit to Mao's tomb led him to express a thankful farewell to the days of the Great Helmsman (17). The growing materialism of Chinese society was evident in the changes in youth culture described by Beverley Hooper (18) and in the increasing westernization of the region around Canton noted by Orville Schell (19).

Claudie Broyelle's doubts about the success of the women's movement in China were supported by Margery Wolf. She accepted that there had been real improvements in the material quality of women's lives, but her research convinced her that nothing resembling the revolutionary emancipation of women had occurred (20). The introduction, in 1979, of the single-child family policy was significant in this context. Elizabeth Croll described how the policy was translated into practice in a district of Peking (21). Rosemary Mahoney, an American student on a teaching exchange to Hangchow University, conveyed vividly her conflicting impressions of her time in China (22).

Whereas the 1980s had seen real improvements in material standards, there had been no political progress. The anthology concludes with extracts from the Amnesty International report on violations of human rights in China (23) and three extracts from western accounts of the protest movement, headed by students, which culminated in the massacre in Tiananmen Square in Peking on the night of 3–4 June 1989 (24–6).

1) *Another model for industrialization*
(Maria Macciocchi, *Daily Life in Revolutionary China*, pp. 206–7)

But we saw the most extraordinary example of this in a Canton paper plant which employs 300 workers. The recovery of waste is exemplary. Mao visited the plant in 1956, read the plant paper, and listened to the workers' proposals for re-using waste. I saw an unusual photo of Mao on his visit, in baggy pants belted at the waist and an open-necked shirt, talking with a worker near a machine. The paper factory adopted the principle 'Participate in the revolution by observing the strictest rule of economy, wasting nothing where a technique of synthesis can be found.' Another photo of Mao: he is pointing at a cart of garbage and talking to the workers. I am told that the paper mill manages to save 400 cubic meters of wood a year, and to make 200 more tons of paper with them. Further, by recycling the wood fiber and water used in making the paper, they obtain pine resin and sulphuric acid, which are then used in making synthetic fibers; and now they're thinking of extracting alcohol from liquid waste. At present the wood fiber is channeled underground to the place for recycling. Scraps of paper are immediately taken to a boiling vat which makes wrapping paper from them. The water used in papermaking is boiled too; with chemicals added, and purified, it makes vanilla powder! We were told that the workers have learned not only how to eliminate waste so as to avoid pollution, but how to make waste useful and beneficial.

2) *In the grip of drastic experiments*
(Ross Terrill, *800,000,000: The Real China*, pp. 119–20)

Schools, and especially universities ... are in the grip of drastic experiments. Maoists ... said 'revisionists' led by Liu Shao-ch'i sabotaged the 1958 reforms. These would have made education more egalitarian, and linked it more with the world outside the classroom. 'Liuists' allegedly favored professionalism, competition, overspecialization, and individual ambition. They liked to have 'professors rule the universities'. Exams for them meant 'ambush of the students'. They exalted ... 'Teachers, Classrooms, Textbooks.' Ultraleftists embraced the opposite error ... namely, total denial of the value of teachers, textbooks, and the classroom. The Cultural Revolution, claim the Maoists, fulfilled the hope of the 1958 reforms and set China on the path to a truly socialist education system. It had two principles: unity of theory and practice; education to 'serve the working people'. I went to see how this works.

You wonder at first if you are on a campus at all. Here at Communications University in Sian are people, dressed in conical hats and blue peasant jackets, threshing wheat (eighty thousand catties were produced on campus this year). In the Middle School attached to Peking National University, girls are making chairs. Next door are boys, helped by 'veteran workers' from a nearby factory, making semiconductors. In Canton at Sun Yat Sen University I found professors tending a vegetable garden. . . .

After two or three years without classes, many universities began again last fall with a small, handpicked enrollment. At Peking University, where there used to be 9,000 students, the new class of September, 1970, numbered 2,667. . . .

These hothouse students are a new breed. None còme direct from Middle School, but only after two to three years at farm or factory. . . . If a would-be student is a 'sturdy pine' politically, and has been strongly recommended by local units, it is not even necessary that he be a Middle School graduate.

3) *Multiple mothering at the Peking Handicraft Factory*
(Ruth Sidel, *Women and Child Care in China*, pp. 92–4, 96–7)
One of the advantages for women working in the factory is that they can bring their newborn babies to the factory's nursing room when they return to work after maternity leave. The nursing room is upstairs on the fourth floor of the large building here. When we visited late one afternoon, there were twenty-seven babies in the nursing room and four adults caring for them. . . .

The four adults in the nursing room – dressed in white coats and called 'Auntie' by the children – lost none of their aplomb when I was shown in, asked many questions, peered down at the very cute sleeping babies, taking notes all the while. The babies in this nursing room ranged from fifty-six days to a year and a half. Most of the children seemed to be under eight months, though there were a few babies about one year old in playpens at the front of the room. The aunties corroborated that most mothers breast-feed their babies and come in twice during the day to do this; if the babies need more to eat, the aunties supplement with a bottle.

There were few toys in evidence, but the children who were awake were two to a playpen and two to a bamboo carriage, so they had each other for company. Some of the babies slept in cribs and some in carriages. When I asked what was done when the babies cried, I was told that they cannot be picked up, as there are too many; instead, the aunties wheel them back and forth in the carriages. Occasionally, however, they do pick one of the children up. The rather dark, dismal-looking room, painted as many of these rooms are, green from the floor to about halfway and white the rest of the way to the ceiling, was in direct contrast to the very pretty, multicolored clothes, supplied by the parents, that the children were wearing. . . .

I wondered how the aunties were chosen. They told me that they were chosen from among the workers in the factory who are the 'most responsible and the most patient'. They have no special training.

Noticing the cement floor, nearly every square inch of which was covered with cribs, playpens, and carriages, I wondered if, as the children get older, they have an opportunity to walk around the nursing room. We were told that either they walk in a walker or the mother takes the child outside at lunchtime for a walk, but they do not walk on the floor, because it is 'dirty'. I had heard other aunties show the same concern over dirt and restrict children's mobility because of it. Here, as in other nurseries, they take the children's fingers out of their mouths because 'their fingers are dirty'. The children do not cry when their fingers are taken out of their mouths. And we saw no evidence of the use of pacifiers.[. . .]

Toilet training is collective and is begun at a year or a year and a half. . . . After breakfast the children sit on white enamel potties and all have their bowel movements together! In another nursing room we visited, we were told that the children all sit on potties after lunch as well. Chinese children are expected to be trained by the age of eighteen months, but if they are not, the teachers in the nursery to which they go at a year and a half will help them. I did not have the feeling that toilet-training was an area of particular difficulty; adults were matter-of-fact when I talked with them about it and seemed to feel it was all fairly routine.

4) *What is holding China together?*
(Jan Myrdal, *China: The Revolution Continued*, pp. 190–1)
It was with the cultural revolution that Mao Tse-tung Thought really reached the entire Chinese people. And it was with this thinking that the people launched their attack on the political apparatuses which had begun to fossilize into institutions of privilege.

Now *Quotations from Chairman Mao Tse-tung* is found in every home in China. In most homes out in the countryside it is the first book the house has ever owned. Everyone is reading it or having it read aloud. It is no formal or ritualized reading, as of a catechism. In all discussions – How much manure? Where shall we invest? How solve the irrigation problem? – they start with Mao Tse-tung. In every question people are proceeding by discussion. No order, no decision from 'above' is accepted without question. People are examining and discussing the contents of such decisions before implementing them. And in these discussions everyone has to take part and give his or her opinion.

What is holding China together is not an administrative apparatus. The apparatus has been cut down. And is still being cut down. It has a function, has its tasks to perform; but to decide China's destiny and be an abode of decision-makers is not one of them. [. . .]

What is holding China together is the discussion of Mao Tse-tung Thought. And that is why it is also correct to say that the fields are yielding better harvests because people's ways of thinking have been changed.

5) *Transformations in the social division of labour*
(Charles Bettelheim, *Cultural Revolution and Industrial Organization in China*, pp. 78–80)
The division between manual labor and intellectual labor in a capitalist factory is reflected in the distinction between the immediate production work assigned to the workers and the tasks of the engineers and technicians who supervise production. . . . When this division is maintained or grows sharper . . . it places the immediate producers in a subordinate position with respect to the engineers and technicians. The transformations that occurred during the Cultural Revolution signify that a struggle is being waged in China to eliminate this aspect of the division of labor as well.[. . .]

The old forms of the division of labor are obviously still far from completely shattered. Certain kinds of work are more attractive than others, but the less appealing jobs are increasingly being integrated into collective tasks which enable each individual to play a clearly useful and active role. . . . The effort to make work less fragmentary by modifying its conditions and enabling each worker to master part of the production process is also very important. The assembly line must not dominate the worker; increasingly, it is the worker who is setting its pace.

The process of revolutionizing the mode of work is of necessity a long one – but it has been partially initiated through recognition of the fact that specific forms of the division of labor do not result from an a abstract development of the productive forces, but that a work mode results from a transformation of the relations of production by past or present class struggles.

The transformations designed to eliminate the division between manual labor and intellectual labor are of decisive importance in achieving progress along the road to socialism. Generally speaking, they signify that one of the most profound characteristics of all class societies – the social separation between theory and practice – is . . . being eliminated.

6) *Nixon's trip to China*
(Henry Kissinger, *The White House Years*, pp. 1055–6)

On arrival at the Presidential guest house, the entire party was seated in easy chairs arranged in a circle. . . . Chou [En-lai] led a friendly, bantering conversation in which, as always, he managed to pay attention to every member of the American party.

In this manner Nixon was exposed for the first time to the Chinese style of diplomacy. The Soviets tend to be blunt, the Chinese insinuating. The Soviets insist on their prerogatives as a great power. The Chinese establish a claim on the basis of universal principles and a demonstration of self-confidence that attempts to make the issue of power seem irrelevant. The Soviets offer their goodwill as a prize for success in negotiations. The Chinese use friendship as a halter in advance of negotiation; by admitting the interlocutor to at least the appearance of personal intimacy, a subtle restraint is placed on the claims he can put forward. The Soviets, inhabiting a country frequently invaded and more recently expanding its influence largely by force of arms, are too unsure of their moral claims to admit the possibility of error. They move from infallible dogma to unchangeable positions. . . . The Chinese, having been culturally preeminent in their part of the world for millennia, can even use self-criticism as a tool. The visitor is asked for advice – a gesture of humility eliciting sympathy and support. This pattern also serves to bring out the visitor's values and aims; he is thereby committed, for the Chinese later can (and often do) refer to his own recommendations. The Soviets, with all their stormy and occasionally duplicitous behaviour, leave an impression of extraordinary psychological insecurity. The Chinese stress, because they believe in it, the uniqueness of Chinese values. Hence they convey an aura of imperviousness to pressure; indeed, they preempt pressure by implying that issues of principle are beyond discussion.

In creating this relationship Chinese diplomats, at least in their encounters with us, proved meticulously reliable. They never stooped to petty maneuvers; they did not haggle; they reached their bottom line quickly, explained it reasonably, and defended it tenaciously. They stuck to the meaning as well as the spirit of their undertakings. As Chou was fond of saying: '*Our* word counts.'

Every visit to China was like a carefully rehearsed play in which nothing was accidental and yet everything appeared spontaneous. The

Chinese remembered every conversation.... On my ten visits to China, it was as if we were engaged in one endless conversation with an organism that recalled everything, seemingly motivated by a single intelligence. This gave the encounters both an exhilarating and occasionally a slightly ominous quality. It engendered a combination of awe and sense of impotence at so much discipline and dedication – not unusual in the encounter of foreigners with Chinese culture.

And so it was on Nixon's visit. By the time we had taken tea, all present felt convinced – just as I had seven months earlier during my secret visit – that they had been admitted into a very exclusive club, though there had yet to take place a single substantive conversation.

7) *Very little difference between rich and poor*
(J.K. Galbraith, *A China Passage*, pp. 135–6)
... Somewhere in the recesses of the Chinese polity there may be a privileged Party and official hierarchy. Certainly it is the least ostentatious ruling class in history. So far as the visitor can see or is told, there is – for worker, technician, engineer, scientist, plant manager, local official, even, one suspects, table tennis player – a truly astonishing approach to equality of income. Older skilled workers, doctors and professors retain the higher incomes, rising to as much as Y300 or roughly U.S $150 a month.... But with age and retirement these higher incomes are being phased out. A younger generation from apprentice to plant manager is in the range from Y35 to a maximum of Y100 or Y150 a month, or roughly from $17 to $50 or at the very most $75. In agriculture, as noted, incomes are less. Since food and basic clothing are cheap, housing costs nominal and medical care mostly free, these are not starvation wages. The urban standard of living includes a bicycle, a watch and, in the few houses we saw, a sewing machine. In each excursion group thronging the parks and public monuments there is at least one camera. People reach places of work and recreation by public transportation that is cheap and looks efficient. Clearly there is very little difference between rich and poor.

8) *The ease of equality*
(Shirley MacLaine, *You Can Get There from Here*, pp. 239–40)
In retrospect, I believe that the fundamental problem *all* of us were having in China had to do with the image we had of ourselves as women.

What influenced us most in China, beyond economic progress, or food production, or the organized unity of the masses, or even how pleasant the Chinese were to each other, was how the *Chinese women* behaved with the *Chinese men*. There it was, on a primitive and fundamental level. *The ease of equality*. We saw it all around us every day. The Chinese women were dressed in nondescript, unisex clothes, with no make-up, no jewelry, no professional hair-styling. They had none of the traditional feminine fripperies. Yet, precisely because they were not preoccupied with such things, they appeared secure in their femininity and there was a lovely ease in their relationships with men.

We saw arguments and disagreements between husbands and wives, or co-workers, male and female, or students, but sex was never a factor. There were no flirtatious glances or hostile putdowns woven into the arguments. The *subject* of the disagreement was more important than how the argument was conducted.

The Chinese women didn't seem to want to be 'better' than men, or 'as good as men.' They were more interested in extending *themselves* to the limits of their own capacities.... There was no evidence of the kind of sad power game that some of our women find themselves playing so often.

9) *The model brigade*
(Simon Leys, *Chinese Shadows*, pp. 74–5)
In the Maoist religion, which teaches that spirit dominates matter and that revolutionary will by itself can move mountains, Tachai is a holy place and is for the faithful a kind of Lourdes or Fatima. China is covered with inscriptions that repeat: 'Let us learn from Tachai!' Since eight hundred million Chinese must model themselves on the six hundred inhabitants of Tachai, the task of these last seems to have been reduced to bearing their own holiness, as a monstrance, under the gaze of the myriads of pilgrims who trundle daily to the miraculous village. Since part of the herculean labors said to have been done by the peasants with their bare hands was in fact done by the army, and since the other Chinese villages can hardly hope for such help, one realizes that the model offers to its imitators a rather discouraging perfection.

... I had the chance to visit Tachai with a cosmopolitan group of foreigners, piloted through China by officials from the Ministry of Foreign Affairs. The village headman, whose photograph is nearly as common in China as Mao's, was there for once (he spends most of his time travelling around the country, taking part in conferences and other bureaucratic activities) and he gave us a banquet. For this occasion he came with his head wrapped in a carefully knotted towel, which in the fields under a glaring sun would be useful for wiping the sweat away but at an official gathering or other social occasion becomes something like the feathered headdress of an Apache chief selling souvenirs to tourists. This operetta peasant dress was balanced by the proletarian-postcard disguise of some of the Foreign Affairs officials: one of them, who as a rule wears impeccably cut Sun Yat-sen jackets, came down the first morning in old clothes, artistically patched and rumpled, which he had kept in his suitcase for the visit to the Holy Places. The lodging house at Tachai had subtle rustic touches: international capitalists and other tourists who 'do' China are like Marie Antoinette playing at being a shepherdess; the meals are no less delicious or less abundant than in the Peking, Canton, or Shanghai palaces for foreigners, but here they are touched with a well-studied primitivism, a shrewd naïvety. In the usual vast array of dishes, some dissonant notes are skillfully struck – a dozen hard-boiled eggs on a tin plate here, a bowl of gruel there – and added to the usual choice of wines, beers, soft drinks, and alcohol is a fearful local spirit. The gourmet brave enough to taste it is suddenly drenched in sweat, giving him the virile and exalting sense that he is somehow communing with the hard task of building socialism.

10) *On the cult of Chairman Mao*
(Claudie Broyelle, *China: A Second Look*, pp. 204–5)
We will begin by detailing here a few items which, although common knowledge throughout China, are – quite fortuitously, of course – somewhat less familiar in pro-Chinese quarters in France.

In some organisations, when answering the telephone, instead of just stupidly saying 'Hello!'. . . it was far better to say, not actually 'Heil Mao!', but 'Long live Chairman Mao!', a distinction which of course entirely eliminates the possibility of any confusion with another system, another country, another time. [. . .]

You could have been thrown into jail at that time for wrapping up your peelings in a newspaper, had you not previously cut out of it all the photos of the Great Helmsman (though if you had, there'd have been nothing left of the paper).

It seems that all this has been criticised; today the cult is at an end. Certainly stall owners will wrap your fish up for you in the *Renmin Ribao* without cutting out the Chairman's photos, but the pages are still covered with them. What goes on page one on all national holidays? His photo. And what holidays are celebrated? Not the Chairman's birthday (that would be personality cult), but the date of publication of each of his major works. [. . .]

At the end of 1973, in the No. 2 Foreign Languages Institute in Peking, as in the whole of China, the extreme right wing essence of Lin Piao's line was being 'criticised'. Trenchant criticism, as the following text bears witness. A text which the administration wanted all first year French students to learn by heart and recite:

'The sun is red,
The sun is bright,
The sun is Chairman Mao,
The sun is the Chinese Communist Party,
Long live Chairman Mao!

Our country is a great country,
We love our great country.
Our people is a great people,
We love our great people.
Our army is a great army,
We love our great army.
Our Party is a great Party,
We love our great Party.'

Our own blindness, the blindness of the European Maoists, was immense in this regard. I can remember the trip which a number of us took to China in 1967. That first morning in the hotel, before going out on a tour, the guides, interpreters, and political cadres sat round with us. One of them announced: 'Today, before starting the day, we will read together some quotations from Chairman Mao, *The Little Red Book*, p. 35, first quotation.'

And altogether, in chorus, we began to intone aloud, some in Chinese, some in French. Not one of our group wavered. And yet it would have been quite enough for one of us to have closed his book politely, put it down, and crossed his arms, for the whole problem to explode in our midst, but there wasn't one of [us] who wanted to seem to be shocked. What a sorry sight the Maoist mass was. . . .

11) *Political Myths: Peasants, Progress and the 'New China'*
(Steven W. Mosher, *Broken Earth*, pp. 302–3)
But it was not until an encounter with the old gravedigger of neighboring Sandwharf Brigade that I was led to reexamine my presuppositions in earnest. . . .

On this particular day, I had gone out to the burial grounds. . . . The grave of the grandmother of the several family heads was to be opened, her bones gathered up and laid out on a large sheet of red paper for worship, and then reinterred upright in a large pottery urn called a 'golden pagoda,' the miniature crypt that would be her final resting place. In it, she would sit cross-legged in above-ground alignment with the beneficent geomantic forces of the earth dragons, which would thus flow to her descendants.

The gravedigger, a wizened scarecrow of a man, had already dug down to a depth of about 4 feet by the time we arrived, and as I watched, his spade began to uncover the top of the casket. The wood had partially rotted away, but he was still able to pry up the lid in nearly one piece. Then, crouching and working his hands through the damp, moldy earth underneath, he began to come up with pieces of bone itself – a knobbed length of thigh-bone, a few odds and ends of vertebrae and such, and then a nearly intact skull. I asked him a few questions as he dug, but he took little notice, mostly just mumbling to himself. One of the deceased's grandsons told me in a quiet aside that the grave-digger was a 'liquor-ghost,' the local expression for wino. . . .

'My, look what we have here,' the gravedigger clucked loudly, and everyone turned to regard the long bronze-colored spike that he was clutching in the air. . . . 'Look at these beautiful casket spikes,' he said, digging out a couple more as he spoke. 'These spikes are real copper. This is an old grave. They don't use spikes like this anymore. Now they just use cheap iron nails that rust away in a year or two. And look at this wood. Forty years in the ground and still not rotted away, not like the cheap caskets that we use now. In the old days, people used to have more money. I would get a thick "red envelope" for each funeral, enough sometimes to buy a month of rice. Now I'm lucky to get 5 *rmb*.'

While everyone, including myself, listened in stunned silence, he turned to me and said, 'You want to know what has changed. I'll tell you. Since the revolution things have been real bad. We have to eat "black rice" [rice of low quality]. We have to wear cheap, rationed cloth.' Then with a curse he concluded, 'Even the rice liquor is not as good as it used to be.'

12) *Industrial pollution*
(Vaclav Smil, *The Bad Earth*, p. 105)

Guilin, in northern Guangxi, is the center of perhaps the most famous picturesque landscape in China. To many Chinese, and to an increasing number of foreigners who fly in, this is the most beautiful scenery the country offers. . . . Yet this is a badly flawed wonderland, although I have been surprised how many tourists appear to notice nothing awry. Plenty is.

The first public disclosures came in February 1979, telling of the Li Jiang being so heavily polluted by phenol, arsenic, chlorides, and cyanide that three factories had to be closed down and the operation of another one suspended. However, these measures came too late for most of the cormorants traditionally used for fishing on the river. . . .

In spite of the closing of the three polluting enterprises (a power plant, a smelter, and a paper pulp factory), and in spite of a government allocation of ¥7.83 million for control equipment, the pollution of the Li Jiang was worse in the spring of 1980 than in early 1979. Oil slicks and white scum floated on the surface, and the stench of the river . . . was 'overwhelming'.

13) *Extraordinary changes in a Szechwan village*
(Stephen Endicott, *Red Earth*, pp. 211–13)

When I returned to MaGaoqiao for a third visit in the summer of 1986 I found the village continuing to prosper. The *per capita* annual disposable income at 500 yuan had about doubled since 1980 and almost half the families had built new brick and tiled houses. With living standards rising the majority of peasants were clearly satisfied with the current policies.

It was time to reflect on the extraordinary changes that had occurred in the village since I first arrived in the winter of 1980. . . .

During my first visit the village was known as No. 8 Brigade in Junction People's Commune; the people worked in collective groups under the production teams and were proud of the co-operative medical clinic, the school, the electrified grain processing mill, the big tractors, the methane gas pits by the side of every house and other tangible achievements. The socialist collective period clearly had been a time of qualitative change in productive capacity, highly successful in turning surplus labour into capital for economic growth. . . .

There was also evidence that the collective period had dealt strong cultural shocks to old ways of thinking and behaviour. Not sufficient to consolidate socialist values in an irreversible way, but enough to have an on-going impetus for equality, social justice, women's emancipation.

Collectively the community found itself with much improved educational and medical services and the healthy appearance of the population was noteworthy. No more drug addiction, no more extended bellies from snail fever.

By 1980 overcrowding on the land was exacerbated. The birth rate had been checked but the large youthful cohort under the age of twenty-five meant greater population pressures. . . . Individual living standards, in terms of housing and available consumer products, had not changed much in two decades. . . .

When I returned to Shifang county three years later, in 1983, sweeping changes had occurred. The signboard of the township replaced that of the People's Commune, while No. 8 Brigade had reverted to its former name before the land reform of 1952 – MaGaoqiao.

People no longer worked in collective groups for work points. The family household acted as the basic accounting unit and contracted land from the production team. Mao's dogged opposition to individual farming had finally been overcome. Under the new system each family worked the land, fulfilled its obligations to the state and to the collective, and then kept the rest of its production for its own use or to sell on the market. . . . The security of the basic food supply, 'the iron rice bowl', was discarded. [. . .]

The village showed signs of a new prosperity. Eighteen families in No. 5 production team had built new houses; there were more bicycles, even a few private television sets. One of the cadres dismissed the former commune structure as 'an empty framework', a remark that would have been unthinkable in the area two years earlier.

It brought one up with a jolt. Why, I wondered, did the Communist Party which had laboured so hard for a generation to bring individual peasant families into co-operatives, now seem bent on doing the opposite? Why the wholesale flight from collectivism?

Conversations with local cadres showed that there were no clear answers; they had not made up their minds about the implications of the new policies. For four years, until 1982, Shifang county resisted the pressure for decollectivization and it was still a time of tentativeness and experimentation. [. . .]

Two-and-a-half years later, on my third visit to MaGaoqiao, in 1986, a subtle change appeared in the atmosphere. Priorities had shifted again. . . . Once again, but without much fanfare, the emphasis of government policy encouraged co-operatives and collective enterprises.

14) *Going through the back door*
(Fox Butterfield, *China: Alive in the Bitter Sea*, pp. 140-1)
Most examples of the back door are more mundane, simple everyday arrangements by which individuals as well as factories, communes, and offices cope with the centrally planned economy, using their ingenuity to coax, wheedle, or procure items and services that are normally unavailable. . . .

I recall one afternoon . . . a Peking journalist I knew called to invite me to a film. When I asked her what the name of the film was, Ling said she didn't know. All she could tell me was that a friend of hers, who had given her the tickets, promised it was an American film. It would also be a *neibu*, literally 'an internal', or restricted, show not intended for the public. [. . .]

Afterwards I asked Ling, a brusque, determined, middle-aged woman who had recently treated herself to a permanent in a beauty shop, how she had got the tickets. 'Through the back door,' she replied. A man she knew who worked for Peking Television desperately wanted to find a new apartment . . . and Ling had introduced him to one of her relatives who was an official in the city housing office. In return, from time to time he gave her tickets to private films. Another evening, she recalled with a chuckle, the film was *The Red Nuptials*, a French soft-porn film. . . .

Ling's tickets to these films were classic back-door deals. As Chinese friends described the workings of the back door, these exchanges usually do not involve money. That would be considered bribery and therefore illegal. Instead they are based on the traditional use of *guan-xi*, the cultivation of contacts and connections among friends, relatives, and colleagues. The longer I stayed in Peking, the more I sensed that almost anything that got done went through the back door.

15) *Rail travel in China*
(Elizabeth Morrell, *A Visitor's Guide to China*, p. 84)
Travelling by train in China is a must for the first-time visitor, particularly for those who yearn nostalgically for the age of steam; the atmosphere of excitement and adventure is enhanced by the rousing martial music often played as the train pulls out of the station. There are two categories on Chinese trains – hard and soft class – and there is usually one soft-class carriage per train.

Foreign visitors, high-ranking Chinese officials and army personnel travel in soft class, which is equivalent to western first class. If you are travelling overnight, accommodation in soft class will be in four-berth compartments with quilt and bedding, adequate space for luggage, lace curtains, and supplies of boiled water for making tea. An electric fan keeps the compartment cool in summer, and the trains are usually well heated in winter. Washing and toilet facilities are situated at either end of the carriage.

In hard class people travel for several days sitting on benches, or they may be privileged enough to obtain a bunk berth – the bunks are three-tiered and the sleeping compartments are open. Among visitors, usually only foreign students and overseas Chinese will be called upon to travel hard class.

16) *The changing face of tourism*
(F.M. Kaplan and A.J. de Keijzer, *The China Guidebook*, p. 98)
As the latest in modern hotels are placed into service for top dollar, the training of staff has failed to keep pace with demand. Being booked into the newest hotels . . . has not been a guarantee of good service. In the Australian-built Jiashan in Guilin we discovered Royal Doulton bathroom fixtures and a color TV and small refrigerator in every room. However, dining room service was snail-like and butter and jam were out of stock for the entire three-day stay of one tour group. . . .

Much of the problem lies in a culture gap between a world of abundance and a world of poverty. The Chinese hotel clerk who makes the equivalent of about US$30 a month shows a room that will cost more than that for a single night; its foreign occupant, moreover, probably makes twice that amount in an hour. An old farmer poses for a photograph; his annual income is considerably less [than] the price of the tourist's camera. The citizens of a country where scrap paper and rags are sedulously collected and recycled are expected to respond to the 'needs' of those who casually discard used refrigerators and automobiles. A busload of tourists eager to return to their hotel after a long, busy day have been refreshed by the soft drinks thoughtfully provided by their guides. When the guides take time out to return the bottles for the few cents deposit, the passengers fail to understand the delay.

17) *This man wreaked havoc*
(Colin Thubron, *Behind the Wall*, p. 37)
The embalmed body lay stiff and shapeless under its mantle, only the head exposed. I did not feel as if I was looking at anything that had been a man. Nestled in its jowls and double chin, the face held a sheen like discoloured ivory. Its eyes were closed, the hair swept back from the high forehead, thin and barely greyed. All that distinguished it were the wide convexities of the cheeks, and a faint, ashy discolouration which spread around the nose and upper lip. Otherwise it presented a heaped enigma. And those who passed by on either side were expressionless too, hurried on by plain-clothes security men. The whole uneasy ceremony seemed to have no heart at all, as if this corpse now belonged only to the terribleness of history. China was already moving away from it. I told myself: this man wreaked havoc and change on a quarter of mankind. Yet I passed in and out of that awesome presence as if through a void. He looked altogether smaller than that. It was strange.

18) *Youth culture*
(Beverley Hooper, *Youth in China*, pp. 19–21)
Like youth in the West, China's young people are beginning to have their own youth heroes and role models: not officially created revolutionary models like Lei Feng but TV and film stars, popular

singers and top sportsmen and women. The star system, a feature of individualistic Western culture and normally suppressed in communist countries, is making itself felt in China. . . .

As the martial music and revolutionary operas of the Cultural Revolution fade into the background, China's youth is developing a wide range of popular cultural interests. There is a growing market, for instance, for the records and cassette tapes produced by Chinese recording studios. (Much of contemporary Western and Hong Kong music is still banned in China.) Local singers like Su Xiaoming sing an array of traditional and modern Chinese popular songs and the occasional foreign song of 1930s or 1940s vintage. The smiling figures on the record jackets and cassette covers are invariably young, glamorous and smartly dressed, with little to distinguish them from their Hong Kong and Taiwanese brothers and sisters.

The songs too are strongly reminiscent of their overseas Chinese equivalents, lilting and rhythmic but without the soft sexy overtones. Unlike many Western pop songs, they are not about personal problems or social protest but beautiful scenery, bright moonlight and happy young people. . . . The occasional hint of a love song is likely to be sung in a foreign language, like Su's rendition of the Japanese song: 'I and you: loving each other, the two of us are together. . . . We'll never be separated. In this world life is so beautiful.'

In large department stores and tiny shops alike, it is young people who cluster around the music counters, gazing longingly at the stereo cassette recorders and asking sales assistants to play the latest recordings.

19) *A coffee shop*
(Orville Schell, *To Get Rich Is Glorious*, pp. 188–9)
While Mao's political ideology still held sway, a Western visitor had no more expectation of finding a Western-style restaurant in a country town like Jiangmen – or even in Peking or Shanghai – than a store that took credit cards or a café where one could sit down quietly with a friend and have a cup of good coffee. Credit cards and coffee were not 'Chinese'. . . .

How starkly the situation had actually changed was brought home to me one afternoon in Taicheng, the county seat of Taishan county in Guangdong. I was strolling with an American friend through a street market where peasants were buying and selling live chickens, ducks, and geese when I thought I saw a sign that said COFFEE SHOP hanging from a distant building. . . . In a moment, I heard the strains of Boy George and his Culture Club blasting out of the doorway: 'Do you really want to hurt me, Do you really want to make me cry. . . .' Inside I found a small, tidy, privately run snack bar with two tables. The walls were plastered with Viceroy, Coca-Cola, and Fanta decals. A Schweppes Tonic poster was pasted on the front of a glass case full of imported Hilton and Marlboro cigarettes. Above a small counter hung a menu, hand-lettered in English, saying 'Western Snacks,' and offering lunch-meat, peanut-butter, and cheese sandwiches. The owner, a pleasant young man, informed us that he had relatives in Hong Kong who had bankrolled his business and kept him supplied with Western snack food. When I ordered coffee, he took a king-sized jar of Nescafé Instant off the shelf, put a teaspoonful into each of two cups, added some sweetened condensed milk, and then poured in hot water from a thermos. As I sat down with my friend to enjoy this afternoon cup of coffee, it occurred to me there was something distinctly historic about finding coffee and contemporary popular music in rural China – although Taishan was an area with much overseas Chinese contact. After so many years of defiant resistance to Western cultural and commercial intrusion, here at least the old struggle had clearly been abandoned.

20) *Not a movement, let alone a revolution*
(Margery Wolf, *Revolution Postponed: Women in Contemporary China*, pp. 272–3)
Beyond a doubt, women participated in China's revolution and believed it to be as much their revolution as their male peers'. A few of them along the way saw the revolution narrowing to exclude those principles for which they thought they were fighting and protested. Whether Chinese women as a whole were not ready for their liberation, or whether, as many feminists now argue, it is impossible to carry out a socialist and feminist revolution together, is now an academic question as far as Chinese women are concerned. Those few feminists who wished to enlist women in a revolution of their own were either silenced or convinced that their revolution must be postponed. But if that revolution is ever to happen, they must be allowed to do as

Mao did, to gather together like-minded people who see the short-comings of the present social order and want to change it. Everything I read and hear suggests that those people are out there, but thus far they are isolated souls only partially aware of their shared suppression. Until they join together, they are not a movement, let alone a revolution.

21) *The one-child family policy*
(Elisabeth Croll, 'The single-child family in Beijing: a first-hand report', pp. 208–9)
Now that she was trained, one elderly and kindly woman, who was herself the mother of two children, was responsible for five courtyards concealed behind the grey walls of a single lane which contained twenty-two households with seventy persons. Of these only twelve were women of child-bearing age, and her main work among these twelve was to keep the records of their family plans, contraceptive use and monthly cycles and generally maintain close contact with them. When a young woman from any of her households registered for marriage, she, as the propagandist, received a card from the neigh-bourhood office which detailed the woman's date of birth, date of marriage, occupation and residence, contraception and her place on the local birth plan. . . . The propagandist checks the regularity of the woman's monthly cycle, her contraception and for any signs of pregnancy. . . .

Of the group of twelve women in her care, four have two children, one has three children and the seven with one child are all in possession of single-child certificates. These latter seven are the 'target' women of her group and the ones over whom she keeps a more careful check. Soon after the introduction of the new single-child family policy she had had to work hard to persuade grandparents and parents that one child was sufficient and that a girl was as a good as a boy. Among her seven single-child families, five had daughters so she thought her work had been much more difficult than that of many of her colleagues. Members of the older generation had often been very reluctant to receive her and were cold and indifferent to her and her cause. Only very gradually had she won their confidence and per-suaded them to accept the policy.

22) *The rat situation*
(Rosemary Mahoney, *The Early Arrival of Dreams*, p. 124)
As we rode down a narrow lane, I saw a woman emerge from her house carrying a live rat in a steel trap. She placed the trap on the sidewalk and matter-of-factly began stabbing the rat through the belly with a long, stiff wire. She glanced idly up and down the street as she stabbed, looking to see what friends of hers were out and shouting hello to those who passed by. Spotless white T-shirts flapped on a line behind her head. The rat squealed and twitched, then lay limp. I was horrified by the sight and looked at Ming Yu.

'I should say the rat situation is worse than the city makes believe,' she said apologetically.

23) *A prisoner of conscience*
(Amnesty International Publication, *China: Violations of Human Rights*, pp. 24–5)
Wei Jingsheng, editor of one of the unofficial magazines banned in 1979, was tried in Beijing on 16 October 1979 for 'counter-revolutionary crimes' and sentenced to 15 years' imprisonment and an additional three years' deprivation of political rights.

Wei Jingsheng, a 29-year-old electrician and editor of *Exploration*, was arrested at the end of March 1979, two days after Beijing Municipality declared a ban on all wall-posters and publications 'opposed to socialism and to the leadership of the Chinese Communist Party'.

An unofficial movement calling for 'democracy and human rights' had developed in late 1978 after a relaxation in official policy had encouraged people to express their opinions and grievances. Wall-posters calling for democratic reforms and respect for human rights soon appeared in the main cities of China. Small unofficial magazines were started which often printed the texts of the wall-posters.

Between late 1978 and his arrest, Wei Jingsheng had published wall-posters and articles criticizing the political system in China and advocating democracy. In December 1978 he published an essay entitled 'The Fifth Modernisation' in which he argued that China needed not only to modernize its economy but also a political modernization: democracy. [. . .]

The trial was not open to the public or to foreign observers although a selected audience – 400 people according to official sources – was admitted into the courtroom. Those allowed in were given admission tickets in advance. Friends of Wei Jingsheng and others waiting outside the courtroom were refused entry.

Short extracts of the trial were shown on Chinese television. However, the official press did not publish any substantial report of the proceedings. . . .

Shortly after the trial, an unofficial transcript of the proceedings was circulated in Beijing. It was distributed at the 'democracy wall' by supporters of various unofficial magazines, some of whom were arrested after a large crowd had gathered to buy copies. The unofficial transcript was later published in Hong Kong and elsewhere. This was the first transcript of a Chinese dissenter's trial to become available outside China.

24) *The Goddess of Freedom*
(Harrison E. Salisbury, *Tiananmen Diary*, pp. 14–15)
[June 2, 1989] We came back through Tiananmen at about 8.30 p.m. The traffic had thinned and I had a better look. Many more people in the square and lots of young people on bicycles making their way there. There were clusters all over the square. Very lively. Many had been drawn out by the appearance of the Taiwanese rock star Hou Dejian, who had joined in with three Beijing intellectuals in a hunger strike. He was sitting with his companions, cross-legged, and singing numbers from his repertoire.

The tent colony was neat, almost military in the way it was laid out, and the Goddess of Freedom – the students' symbol of liberty – loomed high. It was placed rather deep in the center of the square, not just below the famous picture of Mao, as it had seemed in the TV shots.

There was nothing tense about the mood at Tiananmen as darkness began to thicken; instead, it seemed to me rather a holiday atmosphere. Young people hanging out, aimless sightseeing. Going to Tiananmen is the *in* thing. Lots of people, I was told, drop in every evening on the way home from work, just checking to see that it is still there.

25) *Death in the Square*
(John Simpson, *Despatches from the Barricades*, pp. 107–8)
The students sang the Internationale. It sounded weak and faint in the vastness of the Square. Many were crying. Maybe some students had

taken part in the violence, but those in the Square itself had been faithful to the principle of non-violence. . . .

My colleagues and I wanted to make sure our pictures survived if we were arrested or shot, and I told the others we should go back to the Beijing Hotel and come out later. I feel guilty about that now. We should have stayed in the Square. . . . Someone should have been there . . . filming what happened, showing the courage of the students as they were surrounded by tanks and the army fired into them as they advanced. . . .

We didn't. We took up our position on the fourteenth floor of the Beijing Hotel. From there we got the famous pictures that were seen all round the world. Everything in them seemed grey and distant, though. We saw most of what happened, but we were separated from the noise and the fear and the stench of it. We saw the troops pouring out of the Gate of Heavenly Peace, bayonets fixed, shooting first into the air and then straight ahead of them. They looked like automata, with their rounded dark helmets. We filmed them charging across and clearing the northern end of the Square. . . . We filmed the tanks as they drove over the tents where some of the students had taken refuge. . . . We filmed as the lights in the Square were switched off at 4 a.m. They were switched on again forty minutes later, when the troops and the tanks moved towards the Monument itself, shooting first in the air and then directly at the students, so that the steps of the Monument and the heroic reliefs which decorated it were smashed by bullets.

26) *The man who stopped the tanks*
(Michael Fathers and Andrew Higgins, *Tiananmen*, p. 130)

The hero of that day, perhaps of the whole nightmarish week, was a young man carrying a jacket and a book-bag. An American television network later said it had tracked him down, and that he was Wang Weilin, 19, the son of a Peking factory worker. As a column of four tanks drove out of Tiananmen along Changan, he walked into the centre of the road. Arms outstretched, he blocked its course. Miraculously, the convoy came to a sudden halt, the tanks rocking on their suspension. When the lead tank pivoted to the right, Wang moved to block it. It swung back to the left; so did Wang. It was still once more. Then, Wang climbed on to the tank and shouted at those inside: 'Go back. Turn around. Stop killing my people.' Friends rushed from the side of the road to pull him off the tank. The convoy continued on its way.

NOTE

1.   Maria Macciocchi, *Daily Life in Revolutionary China*, London, 1972, p. 1.

CHRONOLOGY

	1900	Boxer Uprising
	1911	Overthrow of the Manchu dynasty and establishment of the Republic
	1916	Beginning of the warlord period
	1919	May Fourth Incident
	1921	Founding of Chinese Communist Party
12 April	1925	Death of Sun Yat-sen
30 May	1925	Police fire at demonstrators in Shanghai
27 July	1926	Nationalists start the Northern Expedition to reunify China
Spring	1927	Revolutionary activity in Hankow
12 April	1927	Liquidation of Communists in Shanghai
18 September	1931	Mukden Incident and Japanese occupation of Manchuria
October	1934	Start of the Long March
December	1936	Sian Incident
August	1937	Start of Sino-Japanese War
	1942	Rectification programme starts at Yenan
August	1945	Surrender of Japan
Spring	1946	Failure of the Marshall mission. Civil war starts again
1 October	1949	Proclamation of the People's Republic of China
25 June	1950	Outbreak of Korean War
February	1958	Announcement of the 'Great Leap Forward'
May	1958	Launching of the People's Communes
	1966	Start of the Cultural Revolution
February	1972	President Nixon's visit to Peking
9 September	1976	Death of Mao Tse-tung
4 June	1989	Tiananmen Square massacre

GLOSSARY

BABOO An Indian with a superficial English education – also applied to Chinese

BORDER REGION Term used to denote area under Communist control during the Sino-Japanese War

BORODIN, MIKHAIL Comintern agent sent to China in 1923

BOXER UPRISING Anti-Christian and anti-foreign movement in north China which culminated in the siege of the Peking legations. Its followers, the Boxers, practised martial arts

BUND Embankment, especially the Shanghai waterfront

BURMA ROAD Road completed in 1938 to link south-west China to Burma

CADRE Translation of *ganbu*, meaning an individual working in an official capacity, who is sometimes, but not always, a member of the Communist party

CATTY Chinese weight, about $1\frac{1}{3}$ lb

CHAPEI Northern area of Shanghai

CHIANG KAI-SHEK (1888–1975) Leader of the Nationalist government in China until 1949 and subsequently in Taiwan

CHOU EN-LAI (1899–1976) Communist leader and long-time premier of China

CHUNGKING City in Szechwan, wartime capital of the Kuomintang

COMMUNES Amalgamations of agricultural co-operatives first established in 1958

CONCESSIONS Areas in treaty ports leased in perpetuity to foreign governments

COOLIE Term used for Chinese labourer

CULTURAL REVOLUTION Name for events in China between 1966 and 1969. The Chinese title for the movement is better rendered as 'a full-scale revolution to establish a working-class culture'

DAN Approximately 133 pounds

EIGHTH ROUTE ARMY Name used for the Communist forces nominally under Nationalist control during the Sino-Japanese war
EMPRESS DOWAGER (1835–1908) Tz'u-hsi, the mother of the T'ung-chih Emperor, known colloquially as the Old Buddha

FANSHEN Literally 'to turn the body over'. Term used as the time of the land reform for peasants standing up and throwing off the yoke of the landlords
FIVE-YEAR PLAN The First Five-Year Plan, in emulation of the Russian model, ran from 1953–7.
FOUR NATIONS LOAN NEGOTIATIONS French, British, German and American banking consortium set up in 1910 to finance railway construction in China
FOUR OLDS Mass campaign instituted by the Red Guards to destroy old thought, old culture, old customs and old habits

GENERALISSIMO Title used to refer to Chiang Kai-shek

HAN Synonym for China, referring to the Han dynasty, 202 BC – AD 220
HANKOW City on the Yangtze, centre of revolutionary activity in 1926–7
HAN-LIN College in Peking entrusted with the compilation of dynastic histories
HSIA HSIANG 'Down to the villages', the transfer of urban youth to the countryside. In the decade before the Cultural Revolution 1.2 million young people were transferred and between 1968 and 1975 a further 12 million

IMPERIAL MARITIME CUSTOMS Service established in 1861 and administered by western officers which collected customs duties on behalf of China.

K'ANG Heated brick bed
KUOMINTANG The KMT or Nationalist Party, formed in 1912

LEI FENG People's Liberation Army soldier whose devotion to duty was cited as a model

LI Measure of distance, about ⅓ of a mile

LITERATI Holders of official degrees, otherwise known as the gentry

LIU LINE Revisionist line attributed to Liu Shao-ch'i at the time of the Cultural Revolution

LOESS Thick deposit of fine yellow wind-blown silt covering large areas of north-west China

LONG MARCH Epic 6,000-mile journey made in 1934–5 by the Communists marching from their base in Kiangsi to their wartime capital at Yenan

LOWDAH Boatman

LU HSÜN (1881–1936) China's most famous short story writer

MANCHU, MANCHOO Inhabitants of Manchuria who conquered China in the seventeenth century and established the Ch'ing dynasty

MAO TSE-TUNG (1893–1976) Communist leader and political theorist

MAY FOURTH INCIDENT Demonstrations in Peking and Shanghai in 1919 to protest against the decision made at Versailles to confirm Japan in possession of former German interests in China

MOU, MU One-sixth of an acre

NEW LIFE MOVEMENT Ideological programme based on Christianity and Confucianism introduced by Chiang Kai-shek in 1934

ONE-CHILD FAMILY POLICY Campaign instituted in 1979 using incentives and disincentives to encourage young couples to limit their families to one child

PEIPING Name used for Peking (Beijing) between 1928 and 1949, when Nanking was the capital

PROVINCIAL ASSEMBLIES Elected bodies first convened in 1909 as part of the dynasty's constitutional reforms

RED GUARDS Youth organizations invoked by Mao Tse-tung in 1966 which played a key role in the Cultural Revolution

RICSHA, RICKSHAW Two-wheeled, man-drawn vehicle of Japanese invention

RMB, RENMINBI Literally 'people's money', a term used for Chinese currency after 1949

RENMIN RIBAO People's Daily, an official newspaper published in Peking

SHANGHAI MIXED COURT Court first established in 1864, which handled cases between Chinese and foreigners. It was presided over by a Chinese magistrate and a foreign consular assessor

SIAN INCIDENT Kidnapping in December 1936 of Chiang Kai-shek by the Young Marshal, Chang Hsüeh-liang, the purpose of which was to persuade Chiang to oppose Japanese encroachment

SINIM Biblical name believed to refer to China

'STRUGGLE MEETINGS' Meetings for self and mutual criticism

SUN YAT-SEN (1866–1925) Revolutionary leader who became first President of the Chinese Republic and creator of the Kuomintang

SYCEE Silver ingots

TACHAI Brigade in Shansi held up as a model of the implementation of Mao's teaching with regard to agricultural practices and the use of incentives

TAIPING REBELLION Mid-nineteenth-century rebellion against the Manchus, the leaders of which professed a form of Christianity

T'AI-SHAN Mountain in Shantung, the most sacred of the five sacred peaks

TAO-T'AI An official: the Intendant of a Prefecture

TARIFF AUTONOMY Under the unequal treaties, China lost control of her external tariffs. The recovery of tariff autonomy became a major objective of the Nationalist movement

THREE PRINCIPLES OF THE PEOPLE Ideology propounded by Sun Yat-sen, the principles being: nationalism, democracy and the people's livelihood

TIANANMEN SQUARE The Square of the Gate of Heavenly Peace in the centre of Peking.

TREATY PORTS Ports opened to foreign trade and residence under the unequal treaties

TREATY POWERS States which had obtained unequal treaties with China

TUCHUN Chinese term meaning military governor translated as 'warlord'

T'UNG MENG-HUI A federation of revolutionary organizations formed in Japan in 1905

TUN-HUANG Site of the 'secret library' and the Caves of the Thousand Buddhas in Kansu province

TWENTY-ONE DEMANDS A series of demands presented by Japan to China in 1915

UNEQUAL TREATIES Treaties signed between China and the West under which China surrendered control over tariffs and jurisdiction over foreigners

WAIWUPU Board of Foreign Affairs

WEIHAIWEI Territory in Shantung leased to Great Britain in 1898

WHITE WOLF REBELLION Rebellion which ravaged north China between 1911 and 1914. Originally opposed to Yüan Shih-k'ai and aimed at restoration of the Manchus. Later supported by followers of Sun Yat-sen

YAMEN Office and residence of an official

YAO-FANG Cave house

YELLOW PERIL Phrase used by the German Emperor, William II, in a speech made at the time of the Sino-Japanese War of 1894–5, to refer to the threat to the Christian West from the Asiatic world

YENAN Town in Shensi, wartime capital of the Chinese Communist Party

YOUNG CHINA Expression used to denote the ideas and the social groups which emerged in the late imperial period and which rejected tradition and favoured change

YUAN Unit of currency: in 1983 £1 sterling was worth 3.30 *yuan*

YÜAN SHIH-K'AI (1859–1916) Military leader and supporter of the Empress Dowager who, in 1912, sided with the Republic and became President. In 1915 he proclaimed himself emperor

YUNG LU TA TIEN Encyclopaedia of the Ming dynasty (1368–1644), which preserved copies of rare books.

BIBLIOGRAPHY

The place of publication is London unless otherwise stated.

CONTEMPORARY SOURCES

Acton, Harold, *Memoirs of an Aesthete*, Methuen, 1948.
Amnesty International Publication, *China: Violations of Human Rights*, 1984.
Arlington, L.C., *Through the Dragon's Eyes*, Constable, 1931.
Arlington, L.C. and Lewisohn, W., *In Search of Old Peking*, Vetch, Peking 1935; reprinted Oxford University Press, Oxford, 1987.
Auden, W.H. and Isherwood, Christopher, *Journey to a War*, Faber & Faber [1938].
Baker, John Earl, *Explaining China*, Philpot, 1927.
Band, Claire and William, *Dragon Fangs: Two Years with the Chinese Guerillas*, George Allen & Unwin, 1947.
Barnett, A. Doak, *China on the Eve of Communist Takeover*, Praeger, 1968.
Belden, Jack, *China Shakes the World*, 1949; reprinted Penguin, Harmondsworth, 1970.
Bertram, James M., *Crisis in China: The Story of the Sian Mutiny*, Macmillan, 1937.
Bertram, James, *Unconquered: Journal of a Year's Adventures among the Fighting Peasants of North China*, John Day, New York, 1939; reprinted Da Capo, New York, 1975.
Bettelheim, Charles, 'Cultural Revolution and Industrial Organization in China', *Monthly Review*, 1975.
Bland, J.O.P., *Houseboat Days in China*, Heinemann, 1909; popular edition, 1919.
Bland, J.O.P. and Backhouse E., *China Under the Empress Dowager*, Heinemann, 1910.

Bland, J.O.P., *Recent Events and Present Policies in China*, Heinemann, 1912.

Bland, J.O.P., *China Japan and Korea*, Heinemann, 1921.

Bland, J.O.P., *China: The Pity of It*, Heinemann, 1932.

Bodde, Derk, *Peking Diary*, Henry Schuman, New York, 1950.

Borel, Henri, *The New China*, Fisher Unwin, 1912.

Braun, Otto, *A Comintern Agent in China 1932–1939*, Hurst, 1982.

Broyelle, Claudie, and others, *China: A Second Look*, Harvester, Brighton, 1980.

Buck, John Lossing, *Chinese Farm Economy*, University of Chicago Press, Chicago, 1930.

Buck, Pearl, *The Good Earth*, Grosset & Dunlap, New York, 1931; thirty-third printing, 1936.

Burton, Margaret E., *The Education of Women in China*, Revell, New York, 1911.

Butterfield, Fox, *China: Alive in the Bitter Sea*, Hodder & Stoughton, 1982.

Buxton, L.H. Dudley, *China: The Land and the People*, Clarendon Press, Oxford, 1929.

Cameron, James, *Mandarin Red*, Michael Joseph, 1955.

Cantlie, James and Jones, C. Sheridan, *Sun Yat Sen and the Awakening of China*, Jarrold & Sons, [1912].

Carl, Katherine Augusta, *With the Empress Dowager of China*, 1906; reprinted KPI, 1986.

Carlson, Evans Fordyce, *The Chinese Army: Its Organization and Military Efficiency*, Institute of Pacific Relations, New York, 1940.

Cartier-Bresson, Henri, *China: Photographed by Henri Cartier-Bresson*, text by Henri Cartier-Bresson and Barbara Brakeley Miller, Bantam Books, New York, 1964.

Chapman, H. Owen, *The Chinese Revolution 1926–27*, Constable, 1928.

Conger, Sarah Pike, *Letters from China*, Hodder & Stoughton, 1909.

Cornaby, William Arthur, *China Under the Search-Light*, Fisher Unwin, 1901.

Cressy-Marcks, Violet, *Journey into China*, Hodder & Stoughton, 1940.

Croll, Elisabeth, 'The single-child family in Beijing: A first-hand report', in E. Croll, D. Davin and P. Kane eds., *China's One-Child Family Policy*, Macmillan, 1985.

Croly, Herbert, *Willard Straight*, Macmillan, New York, 1924.

Crook, Isabel and David, *Mass Movement in a Chinese Village: Ten Mile Inn*, Routledge & Kegan Paul, 1979.

Crow, Carl, *Four Hundred Million Customers*, Harper & Brothers, 1937.

de Beauvoir, Simone, *The Long March*, André Deutsch and Weidenfeld & Nicolson, 1958.

Dewey, John and Alice, *Letters from China and Japan*, Dent & Sons, [1920].

Dickinson, G. Lowes, *Appearances: Being Notes of Travel*, Dent & Sons, 1914.

Dingle, Edwin J., *Across China on Foot*, Arrowsmith, Bristol, 1911.

D'Ollone, Vicomte, *In Forbidden China: The D'Ollone Mission 1906–1909 China-Tibet-Mongolia*, Fisher Unwin, 1912.

Douglas, R.K., *Society in China*, A.D. Innes, popular edition, 1895.

Dunlap, A.M., *Behind the Bamboo Curtain: The Experiences of an American Doctor in China*, Public Affairs Press, Washington, DC, 1956; reprinted Greenwood Press, Westwood, Connecticut, 1973.

Eddy, George Sherwood, *The New Era in Asia*, Oliver, Anderson and Ferrier, 1914.

Endicott, Stephen, *Red Earth: Revolution in a Sichuan Village*, Tauris, 1988.

Farmer, Rhodes, *Shanghai Harvest*, Museum Press, 1945.

Fathers, Michael and Higgins, Andrew, *Tiananmen: The Rape of Peking*, The Independent, 1989.

Fleming, Peter, *One's Company: A Journey to China*, Cape, 1934.

Fokkema, D.W., *Report from Peking*, C. Hurst, 1971.

Forman, Harrison, *Report from Red China*, Henry Holt, New York, 1945.

Franck, Harry A., *Wandering in Northern China*, Century, New York, [1923].

Franck, Harry A., *Roving through Southern China*, Century, New York, 1925.

Freyn, Hubert, *Chinese Education in the War*, Kelly and Walsh, Shanghai, 1940.

Galbraith, John Kenneth, *A China Passage*, Houghton Mifflin, Boston, 1973.

Gale, George Stafford, *No Flies in China*, George Allen & Unwin, 1955.

Gamble, Sidney D., *Peking: A Social Survey*, George H. Doran, New York, 1921.

Gamewell, Mary Ninde, *The Gateway to China: Pictures of Shanghai*, Fleming H. Revell, revised edition 1916.

Geddes, W.R., *Peasant Life in Communist China*, The Society for Applied Anthropology, Cornell University, New York, 1963.

Gilbert, Rodney, *What's Wrong with China*, Murray, 1926.

Giles, Lancelot, *The Siege of the Peking Legations: A Diary*, edited by L.R. Marchant, University of West Australia Press, Nedlands, Western Australia, 1970.

Glover, Archibald E., *A Thousand Miles of Miracle in China*, Hodder & Stoughton, fourth edition, 1908.

Grey, Anthony, *Hostage in Peking*, Michael Joseph, 1970.

Guillain, Robert, *The Blue Ants: 600 Million Chinese under the Red Flag*, Secker & Warburg, 1957.

Gunther, John, *Inside Asia*, Hamish Hamilton, 1939.

Hardy, Revd E.J., *John Chinaman at Home*, Fisher Unwin, fourth impression, 1912.

Hart, Sir Robert, *"These from the Land of Sinim"*, Chapman & Hall, 1901.

Hemenway, Ruth V., *A Memoir of Revolutionary China, 1924–1941*, University of Massachusetts Press, Amherst, 1977.

Hewlett, Sir Meyrick, *Forty Years in China*, Macmillan, 1944.

Hinton, William, *Fanshen: A Documentary of Revolution in a Chinese Village*, New York, 1966; Penguin, Harmondsworth, 1972.

Hinton, William, *Shenfan: The Continuing Revolution in a Chinese Village*, Secker & Warburg, 1983.

Hobbs, Lisa, *I Saw Red China*, McGraw-Hill, New York, 1966.

Holcombe, Arthur N., *The Spirit of the Chinese Revolution*, Knopf, 1930.

Hooper, Beverley, *Youth in China*, Penguin, Harmondsworth, 1985.

Horn, Joshua S., *Away with All Pests*, Monthly Review Press, New York, 1969.

Hosie, Sir Alexander, *On the Trail of the Opium Poppy*, 2 vols., George Philip & Son, 1914.

Hunter, Edward, *Brain-Washing in Red China*, Vanguard Press, New York, 1951.

Hunter, Neale, *Shanghai Journal: An Eyewitness Account of the Cultural Revolution*, Praeger, 1969.

Johnston, Reginald F., *Lion and Dragon in Northern China*, New York, 1910; reprinted Southern Materials Center, Taipei, 1977.

Kaplan, Fredric M., and de Keijzer, Arne J., *The China Guidebook*, Eurasia Press, New York, fifth edition, 1984.

Kates, George N., *The Years that were Fat: The Last of Old China*, Harper & Brothers, 1952; reprinted M.I.T. Press, 1967.

King, F.H., *Farmers of Forty Centuries*, Cape, 1927, fourth impression 1949.

Kissinger, Henry, *The White House Years*, Weidenfeld & Nicolson and Michael Joseph, 1979.

Klochko, Mikhail A., *Soviet Scientist in China*, Hollis & Carter, 1964.

Kulp, Daniel Harrison II, *Country Life in South China*, Probsthain, 1925.

Labin, Suzanne, *The Anthill: The Human Condition in Communist China*, Stevens & Sons, 1960.

Lang, Olga, *Chinese Family and Society*, Archon Books, n.p., 1946, reprinted 1968.

Lanning, George, *Old Forces in New China*, Probsthain, 1912.

Legendre, A.F., *Modern Chinese Civilization*, Cape, 1929.

Leys, Simon, *Chinese Shadows*, Penguin, Harmondsworth, 1978.

Lindqvist, Sven, *China in Crisis*, Faber & Faber, 1965.

Little, Archibald, *Gleanings from Fifty Years in China*, Sampson Low, Marston, 1910.

Lynch, George, *The War of the Civilisations*, Longmans, Green, 1901.

Macciocchi, Maria Antonietta, *Daily Life in Revolutionary China*, Monthly Review Press, 1972.

McCormick, Frederick, *The Flowery Republic*, Murray, 1913.

MacLaine, Shirley, *You Can Get There from Here*, W.W. Norton, New York, 1975.

Mahoney, Rosemary, *The Early Arrival of Dreams*, Macdonald, 1991.

Malraux, André, *Man's Fate (La condition humaine)*, Harrison Smith and Robert Haas, New York, 1934.

Mann, Tom, "*What I Saw in China*", National Minority Movement, [1927].

Martin, W.A.P., *The Awakening of China*, Hodder & Stoughton, 1907.

Maugham, W. Somerset, *On a Chinese Screen*, Heinemann, 1922.

Monroe, Paul, *China: A Nation in Evolution*, Macmillan, New York, 1928.

Morrell, Elizabeth, *A Visitor's Guide to China*, Michael Joseph, 1983.

Morrison, George Ernest, edited by Lo Hui-min, *The Correspondence of G.E. Morrison, Vol I: 1895–1912*, Cambridge University Press, Cambridge, 1976.

Mosher, Steven W., *Broken Earth: The Rural Chinese*, Collier Macmillan, 1983.

Myrdal, Jan, *Report from a Chinese Village*, Penguin, 1967.

Myrdal, Jan and Kessle, Gun, *China: The Revolution Continued*, Chatto & Windus, 1971.

Oliver, Frank, *Special Undeclared War*, Cape, 1939.

Peck, Graham, *Two Kinds of Time*, Houghton Mifflin, Boston, 1950.

Powell, John B., *My Twenty-Five Years in China*, Macmillan, New York, 1945.

Rasmussen, O.D., *Tientsin: An Illustrated Outline History*, Tientsin Press, Tientsin, 1925.

Rasmussen, O.D., *What's Right with China*, Commercial Press, Shanghai, 1927.

Rickett, Allyn and Adele, *Prisoners of Liberation: Four Years in a Chinese Communist Prison*, Anchor Press, Doubleday, Garden City, New York, 1973.

Rigg, Lt Col. Robert B., *Red China's Fighting Hordes*, Military Service Publishing Company, Harrisburg, Pennsylvania, revised edition, 1952.

Robinson, Joan, *The Cultural Revolution in China*, Penguin, Harmondsworth, 1969.

Rosinger, Lawrence K., *China's Crisis*, Knopf, New York, 1945.

Ross, Edward Allsworth, *The Changing Chinese*, Fisher Unwin, 1911.

Salisbury, Harrison E., *Tiananmen Diary: Thirteen Days in June*, Unwin, 1989.

Schell, Orville, *To Get Rich Is Glorious: China in the Eighties*, Robin Clark, 1985.

Scidmore, Eliza Ruhamah, *China: The Long-Lived Empire*, Macmillan, 1900.

Service, John S., *Lost Chance in China: The World War II Despatches of John S. Service*, edited by Joseph W. Esherick, Random House, New York, 1974.

Sheean, Vincent, *Personal History*, Literary Guild, New York, 1934.

Sidel, Ruth, *Women and Child Care in China*, Penguin, Harmondsworth, 1972, revised edition 1982.

Simpson, John, *Despatches from the Barricades*, Hutchinson, 1990.

Smedley, Agnes, *Battle Hymn of China*, Gollancz, 1944.

Smil, Vaclav, *The Bad Earth: Environmental Degradation in China*, Zed Press, 1984.

Smith, Arthur H., *China In Convulsion*, 2 vols., Oliphant, Anderson & Ferrier, 1901.

Snow, Edgar, *Red Star Over China*, Gollancz, 1937.

Snow, Edgar, 'Interview with Mao', *The New Republic*, 27 February 1965.

Stein, M. Aurel, *Ruins of Desert Cathay*, 2 vols., Macmillan, 1912.

Stilwell, Joseph W., edited Theodore H. White, *The Stilwell Papers*, William Sloane, New York, 1948.

Stowe, Leland, *They Shall Not Sleep*, Knopf, New York, 1944.

Strong, Anna Louise, *China's Millions: The Revolutionary Struggles from 1927–1935*, Gollancz, 1936.

Suigo, Father Carlo, *In the Land of Mao Tse-tung*, George Allen & Unwin, 1953.

Taylor, Charles, *Reporter in Red China*, Gollancz, 1967.

Tawney, R.H., *Land and Labour in China*, George Allen & Unwin, 1932.

Teichman, Eric, *Travels of a Consular Officer in North-West China*, Cambridge University Press, Cambridge, 1921.

Terrill, Ross, *800,000,000: The Real China*, Little, Brown, Boston, 1972.

Thomson, John Stuart, *China Revolutionized*, T. Werner Laurie, [1913].

Thubron, Colin, *Behind the Wall*, Penguin, 1988.

Timperley, H.J., ed., *What War Means: The Japanese Terror in China*, Gollancz, 1938.

Varè, Daniele, *Laughing Diplomat*, Murray, 1941.

Vishnyakova-Akimova, Vera Vladimirovna, *Two Years in Revolutionary China 1925–1927*, Harvard University Press, Cambridge Mass., 1971.

Wales, Nym, ed., *Red Dust: Autobiographies of Chinese Communists as told to Nym Wales*, Stanford University Press, California, 1952.

Waln, Nora, *The House of Exile*, Penguin, Harmondsworth, 1931, reprinted 1939.

Warner, Langdon, *The Long Old Road in China*, Arrowsmith, 1927.

Weale, B.L. Putnam, *Indiscreet Letters from Peking*, Hurst & Blackett, ninth edition, [1912].

Weale, Putnam, *Why China Sees Red*, Macmillan, 1926.

White, Theodore H. and Jacoby, Annalee, *Thunder out of China*, William Sloane, New York, 1946.

Wilhelm, Richard, *The Soul of China*, Jonathan Cape, 1928.

Winfield, Gerald F., *China: The Land and People*, William Sloane, New York, 1948.

Winnington, Alan, *The Slaves of the Cool Mountains*, Lawrence & Wishart, 1959.

Wolf, Margery, *Revolution Postponed: Women in Contemporary China*, Methuen, 1987.

Woodhead, H.G.W., *The Truth About the Chinese Republic*, Hurst & Blackett, [1925].

OTHER WORKS

Feuerwerker, Albert, *The Foreign Establishment in China in the Early Twentieth Century*, Center for Chinese Studies, University of Michigan, Ann Arbor, 1976.

Harris, Peter, *Political China Observed: A Western Perspective*, Croom Helm, 1980.

Hollander, Paul, *Political Pilgrims: Travels of Western Intellectuals to the Soviet Union, China, and Cuba 1928-1978*, Oxford University Press, Oxford, 1981.

Isaacs, Harold R., *Images of Asia: American Views of China and India*, Harper and Row, New York, 1972.

Mackerras, Colin, *Western Images of China*, Oxford University Press, Hong Kong, 1989.

Oksenberg, Michael, 'Politics takes command: an essay on the study of post-1949 China', in J. K. Fairbank ed., *The Cambridge History of China, Volume 14, The People's Republic, Part I: The Emergence of Revolutionary China 1949–1965*, Cambridge University Press, Cambridge, 1987.

ACKNOWLEDGEMENTS

As in the case of *China Through Western Eyes: The Nineteenth Century*, I have a large debt of gratitude to the staff of Huddersfield Polytechnic Library who gave me invaluable help in obtaining the hundreds of books which were reviewed for possible inclusion in this anthology.

I must also thank my colleagues, in particular Professor Keith Laybourn, for advice and cheerful support, at a time when pressure of work has ceased to be a matter for facetious comment.

Last, but not least, are the thanks I would like to offer to my wife Jan, for her encouragement and for her help with the proof-reading.

The author and publisher wish to thank the following publishers who gave their permission for use of copyright material. They apologize for any inadvertent infringement of copyright.

Amnesty International Publication for an extract from *China: Violations of Human Rights* (AI Index: ASA 17/11/84), London, 1984; Cambridge University Press for an extract from *The Correspondence of G.E. Morrison, Vol I: 1895–1912*, edited by Lo Hui-min, Cambridge, 1976; Victor Gollancz Ltd for an extract from Charles Taylor, *Report from Red China*, London, 1967; Harvard University Press for an extract from Vera Vladimirovna Vishnyakova-Akimova, *Two Years in Revolutionary China*, Cambridge Mass., 1971; William Heinemann for an extract from Colin Thubron, *Behind the Wall*, Harmondsworth, 1988; C. Hurst and Co. for extracts from D.W. Fokkema, *Report from Peking*, London, 1971 and Otto Braun, translated by Jeanne Moore, *A Comintern Agent in China 1932–1939*, London, 1982; M.I.T. Press for an extract from George N. Kates, *The Years that were Fat*, London, 1967; Octopus Publishing Group Library for an extract from William Hinton, *Shenfan*, London, 1983; Quartet Books Ltd for an extract from Orville Schell, *To Get Rich Is Glorious*, London, 1985; Random Century Group for an extract from Mikhail A. Klochko, *Soviet Scientist in China*, London, 1964; The New Republic Inc. for an extract from an article by Edgar Snow in *The New Republic*, 1965; Routledge for an extract from Isabel and David Crook, *Mass Movement in a Chinese Village*, London, 1979; I.B. Tauris for an extract from Stephen Endicott, *Red Earth: Revolution in a Sichuan Village*, London, 1988; University of Massachusetts Press for an extract from Ruth V. Hemenway, *A Memoir of Revolutionary China*, Amherst, 1977; University of Western Australia Press for an extract from Lancelot Giles, *The Siege of the Peking Legations*, Nedlands, 1970; Weidenfeld and Nicolson for an extract from Henry Kissinger, *The White House Years*, London, 1979.